CELEBRITY
WITNESS

By
Caroline B. Boliek

Bridge Publishing, Inc.
Publishers of:
LOGOS • HAVEN • OPEN SCROLL

Dedication

To Jesus,
My First Love
and to My Mother and Father,
Bill and Roesetta Boliek,
Who Taught Me,
by Example,
the Meaning of True Love

Celebrity Witness
Copyright © 1984 by Bridge Publishing, Inc.
All rights reserved
Printed in the United States of America
Library of Congress Catalog Card Number: 84-71119
International Standard Book Number: 0-88270-572-5
Bridge Publishing, Inc., South Plainfield, NJ 07080

Contents

Introduction v

Part I: Celebrities in the Television and Film Industries
1. Efrem Zimbalist, Jr. 3
2. Bob Turnbull 11
3. Lauren Chapin 21
4. Nick Benedict 33
5. Rita McLaughlin Walter 41
6. Bob Munger 47
7. Susan Howard 53
8. Joan Winmill Brown 69

Part II: Celebrities in the Music Industry
9. Jeannie C. Riley 75
10. Johnny Zell 83
11. Noel Paul Stookey and Karla Sarro 89
12. Danniebelle Hall 95
13. Reba Rambo 103
14. Cheryl and Terry Blackwood 115
15. Andrae Crouch 125

Part III: Talk Show Personalities
16. Art Linkletter 131
17. Graham and Treena Kerr 139

Part IV: A Different Type of Celebrity
18. The Reverend Jack Hayford 151
19. Dorian Leigh 161

Part V: Analysis and Conclusions
20. An Analysis of the Findings 169
21. Conclusions 179
22. Final Comments 183

Special Thanks To:

Paul Hunsinger, Ph.D.
Jackie Mitchum
David Wimbish
Vivian Estep
John Loizidies
Carol Kozma
Tanja Boytar
David Sisson

and to the Celebrities Interviewed
for Allowing Me to Have an
Inside Look at Their Life and Faith

*For What Is a Man Profited
If He Shall Gain the Whole World,
and Lose His Own Soul?
Or What Shall a Man Give in Exchange for His Soul?*
                                    Matthew 16:26

Introduction

The word *celebrity* conjures up various images in our minds. Some think of movie stars while others may think of musicians, politicians or other people in the public eye. But regardless of what image comes to mind, a lot of fanfare and prestige accompany those who are among the famous.

The fact that a lot of people may know who you are does not in itself make you a celebrity. There is a certain specialness that surrounds the famous—a mystique of sorts. Celebrities seem to possess a certain magic that draws attention and admiration. As a result, the public wants to associate and identify with the famous.

Many times celebrities influence the public toward things that are less than honorable. There is an intense peer pressure that deludes the public into thinking that a life style led by a certain well-known person is a stamp of approval for all to follow suit. This kind of power is awesome, but channeled in the right direction, it can create a trend for many to change their way of thinking toward the higher values in life.

The public-relations field has been able to create an aura around the famous. These celebrities are idolized because of the effective use of mass media and other advertising devices. As a result, the public has a tendency to imitate those in the public eye, just as a child imitates his parents.

For the purposes of this book, the term "Christian celebrity"

Celebrity Witness

refers to a person who is well-known, having attained public recognition, and who also professes belief in the Christian faith and principles. The Christian celebrity life style is one that has gone virtually unexamined. Although this life style has received greater attention in recent years, it deserves a more detailed consideration. Celebrities who are Christians have unique opportunities to witness about their faith since their admirers are often eager to know about their life styles.

The celebrities who bear the name of Christ have the unique opportunity to share how their faith has changed their lives. They may be seen as representing Christians and their values everywhere. As a result, it is assumed that the celebrity's public and professional behavior is modified according to personal beliefs.

With the attainment of celebrity status, the Christian is sometimes put in a difficult position, since he will be closely scrutinized and criticized by the public. All celebrities are dependent on the media, and the media will attempt to report in minute detail what they know of the celebrity's secular and religious life style.

One of the major problems that the Christian celebrity faces is the fact that many other Christians suddenly become authorities on how he should live his life. The celebrity becomes a target for unsolicited criticism. Many Christians feel that the celebrity is outside of God's will, since he has remained in the entertainment business. Others criticize the celebrity for taking part in secular shows and productions. They believe that since the celebrity is now a Christian, he should spend his time making an overt witness for Christ.

Because of his influence, the celebrity must be careful about the image he projects. The professional jobs he accepts or rejects communicate an ideal to the public, since the celebrity is often identified with the role or image he portrays.

When a Christian receives the adulation that fame brings, how is his professional and spiritual life affected? How does he make his decisions? How does the celebrity respond to

Introduction

criticism from Christians? Is he or she having a greater witness for Christ by remaining in the secular world or by limiting his work to religious productions?

Celebrity Witness contains an inside look at the life style of various celebrities and their personal answers to these questions. The reader will find that there is a wide variety of viewpoints, but there are sufficient similarities to make some guarded generalities. As all of the information available is evaluated and as comparisons are made, it is evident that the statements made by the celebrities take on new meaning.

Overall, it is the goal of the author to provide the reader with a clearer understanding of the Christian celebrity life style—to depict the problems and pitfalls presented with this status, and the needs that can only be met as concerned brothers and sisters in Christ unite together on their behalf. As the body of Christ works together in this effort, an effective witness can be made to the world so that millions of lives can be transformed.

Part I

Celebrities in the Television and Film Industries

Efrem Zimbalist, Jr.

1
Efrem Zimbalist, Jr.

Efrem Zimbalist, Jr., star of television, film and Broadway, is best known for his role as Inspector Lew Erskine of television's *The FBI*. Zimbalist, 63, is the son of a world-famous concert violinist who moved from Russia to England. His mother was opera star Alma Gluck.

Throughout his growing-up years, Efrem met many of the giants in the entertainment field: Edna St. Vincent Millay, Toscanini, Rachmaninoff, etc. He plays the piano, composes music and is president of the California Chamber Symphony. Efrem studied at Yale and then proceeded to the Neighborhood Playhouse Theatre in New York City. He served in the Army during World War II. Efrem has three children, the youngest of which, Stephanie, has followed in her father's footsteps as the star of the hit TV series, *Remington Steele*.

Zimbalist was reared in the Episcopal church. He comments on what his background was like:

> There were times when I felt close to God, usually when something ominous or threatening hovered over my life. I would call on Him, and He would always answer me. But when the crisis passed, I would drift away. There wasn't a cohesive force. My church celebrated a historical God rather than a living one.

Celebrity Witness

Efrem explains that he had always been looking for something that he didn't have, something that his regular church experience suggested, but didn't quite fulfill. With nowhere else to turn, Zimbalist went into Transcendental Meditation for nine years "to get closer to God."

A bad case of insomnia kept Zimbalist up night after night. When the programming was particularly dull, he would turn to Trinity Broadcasting Network's *Praise the Lord Club* for entertainment. After watching the program for over a year, Zimbalist was finally ready to make a commitment to the Lord. He hesitated to call in to the program because he was afraid his name might be recognized. Zimbalist then realized that if he did not confess Christ's lordship publicly, neither would Jesus confess him before the Father.

It has now been five years since Zimbalist made his commitment to Jesus. He comments on his new faith:

> There are places in God's mercy that encompass everybody on earth. If they make the slightest move toward Him, that's all He's looking for. He is not looking for everybody that checks out. "Yes, I've done this, I've said the Sinner's prayer, I go to church three times a week, I read the Bible." There are billions of people in the world who don't do that and who won't do that as long as they live. They'll die without ever having done it. And I don't believe because of that they'll be condemned. If they know and refuse to do it, then they will be. But if they don't know, then God certainly will honor their intentions.

Until recently, Zimbalist was the only Christian in his immediate family. Most of his family's attitudes toward his beliefs range from tolerance to some hostility. Zimbalist believes his witness is more effective when he can live the Christian life in front of his family rather than trying to convince them verbally.

Efrem Zimbalist, Jr.

Zimbalist is a member of The Church On the Way in Van Nuys, California, where the Reverend Jack Hayford is his pastor. Many celebrities attend this church and they minister to each other. "We are all available to each other, whoever is in town," Zimbalist says. "We are not all there, but whoever is in town will come, no matter what time of the day or night it is."

Zimbalist continues his comments on the ministry within the church:

> We're taught in our church that ministry is throughout the whole body. We all minister and we have to be there to minister. We can't minister to a television screen. It is a one-way street there. We receive. We sit back and we are receptive to whatever goes on, which is okay for a time, but there comes a time when we have to take responsibility, take action.

Often a religious conversion affects a personality's acceptance within the television and film industry. Zimbalist, however, has not found his new faith to be a hindrance in this area.

> I've found a high grade of acceptance in my profession. This doesn't surprise me, because most actors that I've come in contact with all my life have been serious, hard working, family people who have children and work to earn a living.

Zimbalist does mention, however, that most of his friends are not actors. He finds too many "tired egos" in this profession.

Zimbalist thinks that it would be extremely difficult for a young Christian entertainer to make it to the top in the secular field today. He comments that excellence doesn't mean being used in the industry. There are other factors that producers consider. Zimbalist does believe, however, that the future will bring competition between Hollywood film producers and

Celebrity Witness

Christian film producers. He believes that Christians will be active in secular, as well as religious films.

Zimbalist explains how the value system of the secular network operates:

> The policy of the networks is not to make good shows or to make bad shows. The policy of the network is to make money. It's not that they have poor standards; they have no standards.

When Zimbalist is offended by the programming offered, he simply turns off his television set.

There is a positive future for Christian films, according to Zimbalist. But there are a few details to be worked out first.

> One of the things that has to come about for that to be realized is a distribution network [for Christian films]. Movie theaters have been closing right and left, over the country, because there is no product, no family product. There is nothing that a family can go and see today. But if there were a product that the whole family could go and see, the industry would be so healthy. You would have a whole market that doesn't exist today.

Zimbalist believes that television is "God's chosen tool of the twentieth century for world evangelism. To win souls, there is nothing like it." Zimbalist does believe, however, that TV evangelism provides rather shallow teaching. He believes that television evangelism wins souls; but once they are won, a Christian should go to church to get teaching.

> I believe we're called to a fellowship in a church. I don't think a person can ever grow unless he finds that. The way the Lord has chosen us is in a body.

Standards to evaluate particular jobs are extremely important. They can make or break a career, or even more importantly, a reputation. Zimbalist comments:

Efrem Zimbalist, Jr.

I've always had certain standards about the things I would do. I would rather build than destroy. For example, *The FBI* showed an endless amount of crime. That was all right as long as the message of the show was that crime was not a good thing. To glorify, to give any kind of approval to drugs, that is unconscionable.... I've played heavies. Heavies are marvelous. But they ought to have their come-uppance in the end.

I think my own expectations are higher than anybody else's. My own sense of failing against that scale is greater than any I could measure in terms of the public. But I don't despair of that because I know that God is working and He can use me even as I am.

Yet, the dilemma continues. When a job is offered, the actor or entertainer makes the decision on whether to accept or reject it. Zimbalist shares how he evaluates a job:

It is a matter of the largeness of human nature or the smallness of it. The aim is to celebrate the largeness, never the smallness, and that would be so with every villain that I might play. I've played murderers and may yet, probably will. I would only accept the role if it showed that the murderer received and had to receive the punishment that he deserved for the crime. But not to play a murderer, that's idiotic. You can't say the sinners are going to play the murderers, and the Christians the do-gooders. It's ridiculous.

My judgment really hasn't changed since I found the Lord. I have the same criteria as I had before. No, I wouldn't say to the director, "Now, I'm a Christian. I can't drink," because the character is drinking, not me. I don't smoke and I don't drink. I wouldn't like to be that close to smoking again. I'd try

Celebrity Witness

not to, but if the character had to smoke, if the plot depended on it, I'd do it because it was necessary to do.

Zimbalist was closely scrutinized and severely criticized by Christians for portraying an immoral character in the mini-series *Scruples.* But Zimbalist explains his criteria further.

> I don't have control over a movie. All I have is the ability to say I will accept this role or I won't accept this role. First, let me say, I'm not a priest; I'm not a pastor; I'm an actor. When I take a role, it's not to preach; it's to reveal some kind of truth. And, if an actor confined himself only to roles that tallied with the prevailing Christian thought, one could never play Othello; one could never play Faust or Mephistopheles or Macbeth or any number of great roles. One is not trying to preach; one is trying to reveal truth.

Established stars like Zimbalist do have alternatives in certain cases. Muriel G. Cantor, in her 1971 book, *The Hollywood TV Producer,* commented:

> Many important stars have clauses in their contracts giving them consultation rights over scripts. This does not mean full creative control, but they could refuse to do an episode they consider out of character for them, or, in the case of comedy stars, a scene that they do not consider funny. Some stars have the right to refuse to do scenes that make them uncomfortable or that might not show them off properly.

Zimbalist relates the decisions he has made to his faith in Christ.

> I certainly have no intention of offending anybody. I think that is a great sin, and I would never accept a

Efrem Zimbalist, Jr.

role that I thought did that because I am not answerable to these people. I'm answerable to God for the roles I take, and I know what He would do to me if I took that kind of role. I don't need to be instructed by people who write letters.

Zimbalist shies away from fame and adulation. Because of this, he doesn't like to sign autographs, and do things of this nature. He sums up his feelings about his role in life.

It is all right to enjoy an entertainer, it is fine; but to worship, as some people do, is really being misled, because sooner or later they are going to be disillusioned. They are going to be with anybody that they worship.

Bob Turnbull

(Photo courtesy of John Loizides.)

2
Bob Turnbull

Bob Turnbull, former "Chaplain of Waikiki," was a Hollywood actor for 12 years. Turnbull's family paved the way for his future success. His father was an actor on the "silent screen," and his mother was an actress, under contract to a major film studio. Likewise, Turnbull, after he finished college, went to Hollywood and began his acting career. He started on *Matinee Theatre,* a daily, one-hour live television program. Turnbull then went on to appear on such shows as *Hawaii 5-0, The Man from U.N.C.L.E., Petticoat Junction, General Hospital* and countless other television shows. Films Turnbull appeared in include: *Camelot, The Absent-Minded Professor, Tora, Tora, Tora* and *The One Way Out.*

Approximately 14 years ago, Turnbull left Hollywood to start a ministry in Hawaii. Since then he has appeared on Christian talk shows and has worked with people involved in the entertainment world on a professional as well as a ministry level. He appeared on *U.S. am,* the Christian Broadcasting Network's now-defunct early morning magazine show for almost a year as their physical-fitness expert. Turnbull also portrayed the characters of Loring Chase and Tab Barron on CBN's soap opera, *Another Life.* As a result of Turnbull's expertise in the area of health, and his wife Yvonne's expertise on nutrition, the two of them have conducted "Shape Up America" seminars across the country.

Celebrity Witness

Most recently, the Turnbulls have moved to California, where Bob is the associate pastor of a small church and hosts a five-night-a-week radio show over KYMS, Southern California's leading contemporary Christian music station. Although Turnbull is open to what the Lord has for him, he doesn't anticipate working as an actor again. In fact, he doesn't recommend the acting business to anyone, Christian or non-Christian. He explains his stand on this issue:

> The problem with being a Christian in the entertainment industry is that there are pressures and temptations. Any profession has them, but by the nature of being in this field, you sort of prostitute yourself. I don't mean necessarily sexually, but you prostitute yourself on interviews where you're selling yourself. You've got to pump up your ego, you've got to show your talent, you've got to storm in and just take over. You can't do that with many jobs. If you have that attitude, they'll throw you out, whereas in Hollywood you have to do this in order to convince them of a role. So you become your own God. You become aware of your own talents, and that's one of the problems people in the entertainment industry conceivably struggle with.

Turnbull talks about his first experience with the Hollywood life style:

> I went there being a single guy, and being the so-called red-blooded American type. The little ladies and beautiful girls are hanging from the walls in Hollywood. You're thrown against them all the time; and if you're not of a spiritual conviction, you're obviously going to get turned on in a physical sense.

While filming the movie *Dragstrip Riot,* Turnbull became interested in actress Yvonne Lime. She was a Christian and

Bob Turnbull

began to witness to Turnbull. While attending a retreat with the actress, Turnbull accepted Christ as his Savior. His new commitment didn't last long.

> After six months of being a Christian, I junked the whole thing for three years. I just slowly went back down the old grease slide and went back into the pit. I just said, "I can't be bothered. This is more exciting." Then conviction set in. The Lord is patient. Brothers and sisters were praying for me—which irritated me. My irritation meant I was under conviction. I just slowly started getting back to the right relationship with Christ. It took a man of another faith, a famous musician, to turn me around. He pulled me aside one day and said, "Why we Jews don't accept your Jesus as Messiah is because we watch a double-standard life like yours. You talk about a faith and yet you don't even begin to live it. I suggest you shut up and don't tell people you're a Christian. I only speak this strongly because I really like you as a friend." Something snapped when I heard that, so I started the long process of letting go of my life and letting God take over.

Turnbull would have steered his career in a different direction if he had been a Christian when he first went to Hollywood.

> Hypothetically speaking, if I went in as a Christian—first of all, I may not have gone in. Secondly, I don't recommend the acting business to anybody. If I went into it as a Christian, I probably would have done certain shows differently. I would have had more of a trust in the Lord to conduct my career than in my agent. I guess that's the bottom line expression that I should state now. I would have said, "Lord, I'm going to trust more in You to have me do certain roles."

Celebrity Witness

Turnbull tells how he has been able to share his Christian faith while working with other actors:

> I've done nine *Hawaii 5-0's*—nine of those years I lived in Hawaii. But each time I was on, I had an opportunity to witness, or leave tracts or a New Testament with someone. So every time I went on I said, "Lord, there is a spiritual reason that I'm here. Now I'm not going to walk in with a stack of Bibles and look around for the nearest heathen and stick it in his pocket. I'm going to let them start the conversation, which means, 'Holy Spirit, *You* arrange it.'" ... I've given some of them New Testaments. I've followed with a letter. I've given them a tract, etc. All kinds of neat little things like that have happened that have made it very worthwhile. The Lord in charge says, "This is My child. He's going to be on a motion picture set where most ministers just can't walk in." One being a Christian, who happens to be a minister and an actor, can do it.
>
> If I had to do it over again, I would probably be more cognizant of God's timing and power and His guidance of my life as a theater person. A man may think he's manipulating, but the Lord really is. I'd be more sensitive to being there if there is a reason that I should be there. I might just talk to people, share, be open, or just love them if nothing else. While everyone else is lusting over them, maybe I can love them.

Although Turnbull does not desire to return to Hollywood as an actor, he does recognize the rising Christian influence there.

> There's a real resurgence of Christianity in Hollywood, Nashville, New York—lots of believers. A lot of people are coming to know Jesus Christ.

Bob Turnbull

I have no interest to get back into show business at all. Not a bit. With one exception—if an old producer-director friend of mine gives me a call and says, "Bob, you don't have to come in and read. I know what you can do. There's a little part for you. I'd like you to come and be in it," I'd do it. If that came that obvious.

Although Turnbull does not approve of much of today's television programming, he would consider appearing on some of the more wholesome television shows. These programs would include shows such as: *Little House on the Prairie, Bob Newhart, Facts of Life,* and *Magnum P.I.*

I probably could go on some others too, because if you had a lead role, people would know you. You'd be known as a certain person, and your ability to draw people to stadiums and churches and places for ministry would be great. People would be attracted. The methods of getting them there may vary, but the message is the same. We shouldn't be so critical of other people's methods, especially if the Lord's in charge of it.

Turnbull admits that ego can be a big problem when you're a Hollywood star.

We'd go to a personal appearance, and just because we were from Hollywood, people would get fired up. It's a temptation to strut around, to begin to think more highly of yourself than you should. The Bible says pride goes before the fall; and if you start thinking you've got it all and you're very proud of your own self, then I think you need to review what's going on in your life. I've found that I could not, in good conscience, be someplace and start playing an acting role. I'd have to be very aware that I'm a child of the King. I represent the Lord; I'm an ambassador.

Celebrity Witness

So If I represent Him in another area, meaning heaven or earth, then I must conduct myself as He wants me to.

What has been the most difficult thing that Turnbull has had to deal with, being in the public eye?

> As a non-Christian, before I became a believer and was active in some show-biz stuff, I was kind of egocentric, which is a problem that about everyone has to some degree. I misused that importance or that attribute of being attractive to the public or public response or whatever you want to phrase it. I misused it as a social climbing technique or to get what I could and to climb higher in business. As a Christian, that changes.

Turnbull talks about how he deals with the adulation he gets as a Christian.

> People label you. The thing that I want to be is just the way I am; and if some people don't respond to it, that's their problem, not mine. It's hard to do, but there's a real blessed art of accepting praise. I mean, we praise the Lord and He can accept it. When we are praised and we're His children, then we should learn how to accept it . . . . I find it's a growing time for me, when people don't gush. Some of them do in certain circumstances; and then I just say, "Thank you," and I praise the Lord.

Turnbull talks more about problems with ego:

> I think probably the original sin with Lucifer was pride, not the original sin of mankind, but the very creation of evil. So many times through implication and direction in the Bible, it talks about how God hates pride and how He wants us to be free of that. He really wants to destroy that pride and just make

Bob Turnbull

us simple, loving and open. If you're trying to be proud and really up-front and you think you're ever so cool, you may fool a few people; but it backfires.

How would Turnbull suggest that Christians pray for their brothers and sisters who are entertainers?

> The best area is to pray for God's perfect will in ther lives—for God's unconditional love to continue in their lives and that your unconditional love and support and interest in these people will continue. Also, if you read something in *The Star, Midnight Globe, National Enquirer,* those junk magazines, don't necessarily take it at face value. We need to remind ourselves that in the secular court system, people are innocent until they are proven guilty. So the secular courts are more open and honest than Christian courts.
>
> People should pray that entertainers know how to wisely use their funds. Those who are successful are obviously receiving a high amount of revenue. People should pray that they won't be manipulated to misuse their funds. They should remember that God has blessed them, so they should give back the first fruits to Him in the area of tithing and offerings. That's very important. We need to pray that entertainers be protective of their private time, not always so open to the public and that they not say yes to everything. If the entertainer is married, he should spend time getting away with his family.

Turnbull further explains some problems that entertainers face:

> Privacy . . . schedules. How can you build a marriage if you're never together? Being gone all the time and having other things become more important

than your mate and the priority of your family. You've just got to shut it down.

How do Christians hinder other Christians?

> Christians can be the greatest enemies to one another, more than the world can. Some of the worst gossip in the world comes from Christian circles. There is more warmth and understanding out in the world. The reason is that Satan wants to mess things up, and so he'll go to our weakness. That's why he goes to men regarding women and sex. Satan knows the weakness of all men and women, whatever that may be.

What is Turnbull's response to the increasing rate of immorality in the Christian community?

> People ask, "Why is that happening? The Holy Spirit is being poured out into the world." I say, "It sure is, but so is the unholy spirit. It's being poured out into the world too. There's one hell of a war going on and one heaven of a war going on. The two are clashing, and so we're going to have a lot more immorality."

Turnbull is a man of many accomplishments, having written a number of books and having held many leadership positions including his recent appointment as the codirector of the National Association of Christian Singles. His goal, however, is to influence others through public speaking.

> My goal is to be one of the best speakers I can possibly be. I think the Lord is going to have me do a lot of that. I used to do it all the time. I know it's a gift of communication, and if it's a gift, it needs to be returned back to the one who gave it. It's exciting that when you speak, you can influence a life for all of eternity.

Lauren Chapin

3
Lauren Chapin

Lauren Chapin was America's sweetheart in the 1950's as cute little Kathy Anderson on the television series *Father Knows Best*. From the age of eight to fourteen Lauren lived in the fantasy world of stardom. However, her television family was a world apart from the reality she experienced at home. Lauren comments on how she was able to break into the acting profession.

> Both of my brothers were in show business. As far as my mother and father were concerned, they were not actors and had not had a background of acting. I just fell into it through my brothers. I was the youngest in the family, and they had been working for years before I was ever born. Just by chance, an agent friend of my mother's saw the part for Kathy Anderson and asked my mom if I could do the interview. She said yes, and I went out with 150 other people and won the part.
> I'm proud of having been a part of that particular show, having won the awards that we won and putting into society what we put in. The statements we made—I think if television were more like that, I'd like to be a part of it now.

Celebrity Witness

Lauren was ill-prepared for the drastic changes that took place after *Father Knows Best* was canceled.

> I didn't feel bad because I didn't realize what was going to come about. I was really looking forward to the show being canceled. It meant there might be another opportunity for me to do other shows and not be stereotyped anymore. That fell through and I realized that either you are on top or you are not at all. That crushed me. Robert Young went his own way. Elinor went hers and Billy his and Jane hers. There was no unity there and that crushed me. I didn't expect Hollywood to turn its back on me. I had no idea of how to adjust to society, to ordinary, everyday living. I was a workhorse. That is something I love to do, and then when that was taken from me, I was like a fish out of water, floundering. I wanted to be normal, but there was not a normal bone in my body. I just wasn't like everybody else.

The search for personal identity and inner fulfillment was a struggle within Lauren for many years.

> I just felt really lost for about 10 years. I was trying to find my own identity. I was a very curious child. I think Satan uses children like me. I think he really has a playground there because kids are so very hungry and have a great depth of spirit to want to know what life is all about.
>
> I had a head knowledge of Christ from what I'd heard from other people. I never read the Bible much until I got into the Episcopalian religion. I did it then because I taught a Sunday school class. I can't remember exactly when I made a commitment to the Lord, but I know somewhere as a child I did make a commitment. The seed was sown by the preachers that I listened to, but they weren't sown deeply.

Lauren Chapin

There was nothing in my home life to take that seed and root it. Times of adversity came, and when trials came along, that Word was drawn up and there was nothing there to keep me in the presence of God's hand. I just flew to the wind. The devil comes to rob and destroy. He comes to rob the little innocent kid that is not grounded in the Word or the adult that is not grounded in the Word. They do not know who their adversary is, and I didn't know who my adversary was.

Mankind blames God for everything, and I fell into that same position. I blamed God for all those things that were happening to me. It wasn't so much that I blamed God as that I felt guilt. That guilt made me think that God was human and that God was going to blame me, but the Scripture said that God is not a man that He should have to repent. He is not a liar. I didn't realize that God saw me through the eyes that He sees Jesus Christ. I thought that He was embittered toward me, that He was angry at me for having turned my back on Him, and when you feel that guilt, you want to run away from it. That is what happened to me as a child. I just turned away from the church.

I believe that the peace of God will stand forever, and no matter what you put in its place, it is never going to fill that void that you have or that peace that you get when you find the Lord. As a young girl, I was trying to find the Lord and I didn't know that was what I was looking for.

Drugs provided Lauren with a temporary sense of satisfaction to fill the deep void within her life.

I got into drugs. I was just trying to find me. I was trying to find a niche or a place where I could be me and not be Kathy Anderson, where I could just be me

Celebrity Witness

and be loved. I needed to be loved. I thought through the druggies, I was loved. I found that there was a power there that I had never had before and that I could be important. It was a whole crazy world. But through all that crazy world, the Father showed me that He loved me. He put in my path a Dominican brother who I was very turned off to. I was very turned off to Catholics. I was very turned off to religion. I was just turned off, and yet the Father put before me a little brother by the name of Brother Stanley, who was about four feet by four feet. I had met him when I was going to jail. For 6 years he stayed by my side. That man interceded for me, daily for six years. He just shared the love of Jesus with me. He never took his Bible out and thumped it over my head.

It took a year before Lauren would speak out about her new-found Christian faith.

That very first year of my Christian walk, I was a CIA Christian—the kind where you don't tell anybody. I'd just go around being real secretive, but then I got some boldness through prayer. And I wanted to do this and I wanted to do that for the Lord. And every door that I thought was right for me closed, and I said, "Father, what is it?" And one day the Lord said, "Open the Bible." I opened it up and it said, "Don't look to your right. Don't look to your left. Don't look to man, look to Me, for you are My child, you know Me, for I created you. My word is the truth." He said, "I'll teach you the Word of God. You just be a willing subject and I'll be your teacher. Whatever you put into it, honey, I'll bless."

For two years Lauren studied the Scriptures and seemed to be able to absorb very little. However, when she got up to minister one day, it all came back to her.

Lauren Chapin

> I'm in full-time ministry. And I have been for about two years. I travel throughout California and throughout the United States ministering as an evangelist—testimony, the gospel and singing. But my final objective is to get out there and win souls for the Lord and to be used by Him in whatever capacity He wants to use me in. If it's singing or witnessing or preaching or teaching or whatever—I'm willing to do it. I also teach natural childbirth—at home. And I film births and raise two children and three cats and two dogs and now six puppies.

Lauren's ministry often comes into contact with those who have gotten into a rut in their Christian life.

> When I go minister, I see all these churchy people that put on the biggest front. If you were to ask them what the Word of God is, they couldn't tell you. They don't read the Word. They don't read their Bible. I ask them, "What do you do? You come to church for two hours on Sunday and you think that's enough?" It's not. There's more to being a Christian. God puts a trust in you, and you need to live up to that trust, but you need to be victorious. You can't be victorious if you don't have the armor. How are you going to fight a war with just thought? You need artillery. You need foot soldiers, you need a whole battle command out there. God told me that His Word would follow me. God said that He was with me. I'm not alone.

Lauren talks about the most difficult things that she has had to deal with being in the public eye:

> I think struggling with breaking away from that identity of Kathy Anderson and having people see me as Lauren Chapin. Kathy can be a thorn in my side sometimes. It's just working for people to recognize me and what God has given me and how

Celebrity Witness

God's using me. Once I get down from the pulpit, I've had more people say, "You're that girl as far as looks are concerned, but, boy, we know who you are now." And that's a blessing. That really is a blessing. But it's been a long time coming.

Standards for acting roles that Lauren would consider are quite stringent, and she finds it's important not to compromise.

Number one—it would not be a film that had a lot of sex or violence in it. It would not be a horror film. It would have to be family-oriented—a "G" rating. So, you see, there's not too much work out there. I'd like to do a musical like *Chitty Chitty Bang Bang*—that kind of a show. I think those are great fun. Children love them, so do adults.

I have not had a great deal to do with Hollywood since I was quite young. I go back once in a while and do shows. When I do shows, I pick them. The last movie I did was with Gary Coleman called *Scouts Honor*. That was a good family-type situation and I like doing that. There is darkness all around, and I think that we as servants of God need to just reach out wherever we are at and in whatever field. If you are a waitress, minister that way. If you are a street cleaner, minister that way. If you are a teacher, minister that way.

They don't understand what it is that you've got, but they might be drawn to you. The Bible tells us we cannot resist the wooing of the Holy Spirit. When people see the Christ in you, they can't resist that. They want it. Inside they want it. Outwardly, they have a lot of shells and a lot of walls, but God is a strong invisible God, and He can get right through those walls and He can touch even the hardest of people, and He can use the gentlest ways

Lauren Chapin

to do it too. Get right into that wolf pack. Confound the wise.

Criticism and competition within the Christian community distresses Lauren, and she seeks to fight this spirit of judgment.

> We are competing against one another and that is what Satan would have us do. I hear other Christians say, "Well, who does he think he is?" I know the devil has really used that in a lot of Christians—that strike of judgment. We can't tear down the house.
>
> There is a spirit of judgment that is very bad. You know, if God has given you a talent to perform and sing, I think you can sing for Christians and non-Christians. That is what you are supposed to do. I don't think that because you have become a Christian you are supposed to dry up and remove yourself from everything. I don't believe that we should judge one another's actions. If you are in the wrong, God is still going to use you. If He gave you that anointing, He is going to use that anointing. If there is sin in your life and you keep on doing it, He is still going to use you. He is going to deal with you later on, but He is going to use you because He knows that is going to feed His sheep.

Lauren offers advice to those who are aspiring stardom.

> It depends upon their age category. Number one—I do not advocate children being in show business. I have very strong feelings about that. But if you are an adult and you have gone through school and have gotten your education and you have your feet well planted on the ground, I will tell you the pitfalls and tell you to please be aware of them because you cannot serve two gods. You cannot serve our heavenly Father, and then serve

the god of prestige, money and glory. It just does not work that way. When you are a Christian, I think you need to be the strongest and most deeply committed Christian that you possibly can be and not settle for second best. You have a commitment when you are a Christian and that commitment is to live up to God's trust in you. That means if you are going to be an actress, you are going to be an actress that does things that will bring glory to God. I think if people want to be actors and actresses, that is fine. We need them. I don't think that because you are a Christian you should withdraw from the world. I think if God has given you a talent like that you should use it, but use it mindful of Him. Just beware. If Hollywood doesn't give you the right parts, then maybe you need to pray about opening up your own shooting, your own production companies and getting with other talented Christians and doing your own work.

Lauren gives a few warnings about the show-business world to those who feel they are called to this profession.

As you know in any walk of life, you can always find yourself in a position to compromise in one way or another, either by listening to the dirty jokes being said, the slaps on the fannies, little common sexual connotations. It is easy to turn your back and let it slide. In a way, I think it is condoning what is going on, instead of sticking up and saying, "Please don't do that, I'm a Christian and I just don't want you to do that around me." We need to know to speak out like that. That is going to put you on the cross, but you need to be aware that you need to do that. You need to stand your ground. You need to know you've got the greatest force behind you and in you. People are going to respect you. When you are in the world, you are with a lot of unsaved folks. If you are not letting

Lauren Chapin

your light shine, they are going to say, "Why should I be a Christian? She is no different than us." So you need to set an example for those other people to follow. When you are in Hollywood, it is very difficult to do that because there are a lot of Christians out there that are not Christians.

In Hollywood, there are a lot of people that get on the glory wagon and say, "I'm a Christian." So you need to know those pitfalls. You need to see it and be led by the Holy Spirit. Pray each day as you get up and ask God to lead you and guide you in all spiritual wisdom and knowledge. Just continue to give everything to Him, and if a situation comes up, stand your ground. It may mean you'll lose a job. Stand your ground anyway. Because if you compromise once, you are going to compromise again. And in Hollywood you just have to be willing to serve one God and one God only.

Lauren looks forward to a bright future, even though she doesn't know what might be in store for her.

> God knows who and what is best for me, and sometimes what we may desire may not be what God desires for us. And it may not be right for us. I want to wait. I just want to wait on the Lord. I don't want to go ahead of Him. Sometimes people have the tendency to do that.
>
> I look at my life and I say that God has truly blessed me because God has been with me through the height of living well financially and having maids, fine houses, dresses, to the pit of poverty, and I have adjusted well. I praise God for that. I praise Him that I have not been thoroughly destroyed by the fact that I do not have money. I've lived in the slums and I dressed poorly and lived very happily that way. I would always say, "Money can't buy my happiness."

Celebrity Witness

> If I ever get married, hopefully I'll have a home like Jim and Margaret. Because that is what I want. I want that white picket fence. I want the family working out problems together as a nucleus—not singly. I just want that love that flows back and forth. I don't even date. I don't have time. When I do meet single men, I don't know how to relate to them. I am so tongue-tied. I'm like a giddy kid in school.

Wisdom is what Lauren desires most and she offers us her prayer request.

> I'd pray for wisdom in all things. That when I go to minister that I would be wise in leading God's children into all truth and into salvation and beyond salvation into a daily commitment and walk with Christ.

Nick Benedict

(Photo courtesy of John Loizides.)

4
Nick Benedict

Nick Benedict first captured the hearts of American women in the role of Phillip Brent on ABC's popular daytime serial *All My Children.* His performances led to two Emmy nominations for Best Actor in 1978 and 1979. After a six-year stint on the show, he joined CBS and its daytime serial, *The Young and the Restless.* Along with guest appearances on talk shows and nighttime TV series, Benedict became one of America's television heroes.

Nick's acting ability stemmed from a family background integrally involved with the entertainment world:

> It was show business all the way. First of all, my mother was a burlesque dancer . . . and my father was an actor . . . . I stayed away. I took up playing the drums . . . I grew my hair long like the Beatles . . . . Then the Vietnam thing came up. By that time I was seventeen and I was just getting out of high school.
>
> I had started to go to college on a baseball scholarship but . . . I couldn't stand college . . . . I didn't know what I wanted to do. The baseball thing wasn't working out right . . . . I was real frustrated. So I joined the Navy. I thought this would get me out of the house and see if I was a real man . . . . They

Celebrity Witness

> put me on a ship and sent me to Vietnam on an aircraft carrier . . . . I was a bomb loader . . . . I didn't even know what I was doing. . . . I just went in because I didn't want to get killed. I figured in the Navy I would be on a ship and I wouldn't have to fight anybody.

Nick finished his tour of duty in the Navy and returned to Los Angeles where his family encouraged him to try the acting profession.

> My father used to direct nighttime TV. At the time he was doing a show called *Mission Impossible.* He said, "I'll get you in as an extra and see if you like it." And so I worked as an extra . . . . I did that for a year and a half.

Nick worked with such shows as *Adam-12, Mission Impossible* and *Hawaii 5-0.* His interest in acting was blossoming when he met his future wife.

> I met this really beautiful girl, an airline stewardess. And I fell madly in love with her and we got married. We were married four and a half years while I was studying acting . . . . Finally she said she wanted me to quit being an actor and she wanted a baby. I put four years of study into it and I didn't want to leave it, so we split up. That's actually when I started praying. I was twenty-five years old then and I was just real lost. I didn't know what I wanted after being alone for a while.

This devastation led Nick to "The Little Brown Church" in North Hollywood. The church was open twenty-four hours a day and Nick wandered in at two o'clock one morning. He asked God to come into his heart and take over. Nick had had no religious background, but something real happened to him at that moment. Two weeks later he was called in to audition

Nick Benedict

for *All My Children*. He received the role that would eventually make him a star.

> Fame did not come easy. I worked real hard for it. First of all, I had to replace another guy, Richard Hatch. He was real popular . . . . I came in and they said, "Who's this guy?" . . . All I did was concentrate on work. I used to take a character home with me. . . . I was in bondage to it. . . . After a while I started getting all the fan mail, and pretty soon I became the star of the whole show.

All this attention went to Benedict's head, and the fame he received influenced him to do things he now regrets.

> I didn't handle the fame very well. . . . Even though I was popular and all that, I still wasn't real happy. I admit I did get kind of crazy with the girls for a while. I must have gone through a hundred girls in a short period of time.

Benedict finally stopped and evaluated the things he was doing.

> I kind of came out of it on my own. The last three years I was on *All My Children* I decided I wasn't going to go out with girls for a while. I was just going to get into myself. That's when I really started praying again. I decided I wanted to come out of the closet and I did this interview with *Us* magazine. . . . I told them that I'd been praying to God and that God had come into my life. I'd never told anybody about that. My parents got a hold of that. My father asked me if I'd become a Jesus freak. I said no, that it was my own personal thing. He kind of put me down for it, so I never told anybody about that again.
>
> I was still rolling there on *All My Children,* and I let the Lord in, so to speak, a little bit and He let me in a

Celebrity Witness

> little bit. We sort of flirted with each other. He knew that I wanted to seek Him, but I just didn't know how to go about it. I just kept it quiet. I was a closet Christian.

Benedict's life style and values have changed dramatically the last few years. In 1981 he recommitted his life to the Lord when a severe illness brought about the turning point Nick needed. He began to witness actively about his faith after being a "closet Christian" for ten years.

> When people used to say "Praise the Lord," I used to shrug and say, "Oh, that is corny!" but what "Praise the Lord" means is praise the Lord for loving us, praise the Lord for helping us. It's really His praise, because the Lord has His hand on me.
>
> I'm at the point of life now where I want my acting to be meaningful, rather than just be the guy that comes in and impregnates the town, which I've always done before. . . . I would like to keep working as an actor because that's really my forte.

As a Christian, Benedict is now more cognizant of the values that apply to the acting profession.

> When you're an actor, you're an actor. I like to take a role on a soap opera and kind of change it. What they like to see is your own personality in a role. If I become real big again with the soap thing, I think the lessons I've learned will give me more guidelines for my life. I'm not necessarily concerned about the roles I play as long as I work as an actor. I would never go on something that was pornographic or anything like that. There's a code for television, and they always have to show that the bad guy gets it. It's a code of television as far as the networks go. So I would never do that, go on an immoral show.
>
> The only thing I don't like about being an actor is

that you can be out of work for a long time. That's the thing I like about soaps. Soaps can be a six-month, a two-year, to a seven-year run.

I personally got into being an actor because I wanted to have a lot of girl friends. That was my original motivation. Then I found it became a career and then that became my main motivation. Everybody has a different reason why they want to be a star, but I really think it's something you have to give your heart to. You have to be willing to suffer a lot of heartbreak and letdowns. You should be really powerful in the Lord to get through those times. I was nothing until I got *All My Children,* and I got *All My Children* because I prayed about it. Even though I wasn't a Christian and I didn't know anything about the Lord, I just went in there and prayed about it without anybody telling me or witnessing to me. That's the only reason that my career went.

Benedict now hopes he will have a second chance to use his talents and abilities for the Lord.

I would ask God to give me another chance, because I wouldn't make the mistakes that I made before. I've been praying for a second chance to break the bondage because Satan had a hold of me out in L.A. I was broke when I came out of it. I just had to pick myself up and get going again. Lots of prayer. Unfortunately, I had to be knocked down to nothing to do it, but, praise the Lord . . . because I guess that's what I needed. If the Lord wants me to go broke, then there's a reason for that. I don't think the Lord's going to abandon me. He's got His hand on things. God's with me.

Benedict now has a desire to use his influence as a popular actor to promote things that are godly.

Celebrity Witness

> You can use people for your own personal greed, or you can do nice things with that power. You can make appearances at charity things . . . be nice to people and not use people. Especially sexually. You can use women because they hang around TV people. It's evil. You can do evil with the power that God gives you. If you do, I believe that God will take it away. You should always think of that. The Lord's always watching you, and the devil comes around and gives you these thoughts.
>
> For example, "Oh, she's pretty and I think I'll make a move because I know she knows who I am and then I'll just use her and forget her." That's an evil thing. It's like the devil's trying to get you. And then, you always feel the worst afterwards, when it's over, the next day. You feel much better if you resist. That person recognizes you and you recognize them and say, "Hi, how are you? Very nice to meet you." And then walk away. Then you don't go for that lustful flesh. I've found out it's made me much happier to forget all of that, and just think of being a good person and doing good things with any powers that are given me from God. God makes it all happen as soon as you let Him. He'll take it away from you and teach you lessons, too.

With all the fame that Benedict has received, his dreams are relatively simple and uncomplicated.

> I've been thinking a lot about fatherhood lately. Unfortunately, you have to be able to afford fatherhood. I would like to get something going, and when I did, I would like to do good things with the money I would make rather than blowing it, like I did before. To create a life, to carry on the family name. I'm ready for it.
>
> My dream is just to be happy in life. It's not

Nick Benedict

necessarily in my work. Maybe it's because I've reached certain plateaus and been a star and have people recognize me and autographs and all that. I know what that is. I just want to be more happy in my own life rather than in my career or nighttime TV. If that comes, I'll just take it as it comes and handle it. It's going to be real exciting, because whenever I'm interviewed, I'm always going to talk about God.

Rita and Norman Walter

5
Rita McLaughlin Walter

Rita McLaughlin Walter began her career at the age of eleven when she had a role on television's *Watch Mr. Wizard*. She was later a regular on *The Mitch Miller Sing-a-Long* and she was Patty's stand-in on *The Patty Duke Show*. Rita has appeared in Broadway and off-Broadway productions and has appeared in over 200 commercials. She is best known for her current role as Carol Stallings Andropolis Frazier on CBS's number one soap opera, *As the World Turns*.

From the beginning of Rita's acting career, her parents set up a list of priorities for her to follow. God came first, then family, country and finally work. In times of confusion, Rita would look at her set of priorities to see if her job conflicted with them.

How can Rita justify acting in a soap opera where sin is so visible?

> Because the show does not condone the bad behavior. It doesn't say that infidelity is good. The character of my husband on the show was unfaithful. He paid for it. He suffered through it. He wanted to come back and make the marriage right. I forgave him. In fact, I forgave him three times. Then we finally had a strong, happy marriage. It shows that marriages can stay together if you work at it. It applauds family.

Celebrity Witness

Rita explains that *As the World Turns* reveals the natural consequences of sin. Although Rita plays a loving character on the show, she would still maintain her role if the writers turned her character into a sinful, unlikable person, as long as she was seen as the "villain" and paid the consequences for her actions.

> Now as long as they say that sin is wrong, I can play a robber in a movie, as long as the cops win. If they say, "Hey kids, go out and be a robber. That is the way to live life," then I want no part of it.

Norman Walter supports his wife in this view.

> We will not glorify sin through television or whatever. We will glorify what is done right, the way to live and walk with the Lord. We will condemn sin, and if a play comes along and if it glorifies sin, we won't take it. If a play comes along (and it may be secular) which condemns the wrong life, yes, we will take it.

Rita says that soap operas do serve a purpose for those who watch them. First of all, soap operas give people a chance to get out of themselves and to think about other people's problems. Secondly, soap opera cast members serve as a family to people who don't have families. Together, they celebrate holidays such as Thanksgiving, Christmas and Easter.

For the Christian, soap operas serve an extra purpose.

> If you know Jesus and happen to watch soap operas, you can get to know how relationships can break up and how forgiveness rules.

How do people respond to Rita?

> Well, I play a good character, so they are usually very warm. Other bad characters they hit over the

Rita McLaughlin Walter

> head. The good thing about it is that it opens the door for us to tell them about Jesus. They may come to a Soap Opera Festival to meet their soap star. My husband and I travel to churches, and a person may not come to a church function, but they may come to hear Carol Frazier. We get to talk together and then we get to share about Jesus. We hope that Jesus will become a part of their lives, too.

Sadly enough, some Christians don't receive Rita quite as warmly.

> For some reason, people in churches think that somehow God doesn't care about people who work in television. They think that these people are the worst sinners, and that God would say, "Forget about you; I only want Christians to go to heaven." The whole thing is that God came to save the lost. He went to a lost world. The people that work with me are everyday nice people. I love working with them. They don't come in drooling at the mouth or anything, but they are lost and they need Jesus. Where are the people to tell them about Jesus? We need missionaries in every field here now.

Nevertheless, Christians tend to be judgmental of Rita.

> Sometimes we get a lot of criticism from Christians. You feel bad about that because you want to join with your brothers and sisters, but if I just have one chance, one opportunity to share Jesus with people at work I say, "Wow, who cares about what anybody thinks? This is worth it. This is worth it all if these souls come to Jesus."

Rita gives her final comments about working in the secular arena.

Celebrity Witness

> I can now be happy working in a soap opera because of Jesus. You say, "So what? Anybody would be happy working on a soap opera." Believe me, I'm surrounded by people that are miserable, that are unhappy, that are frustrated, that come to me and say, "Would you pray for me? I don't know what to do." They say, "How come you are so happy? What have you got?" So there is a chance to pray and tell them that Jesus is the Lord of my life and He is the reason for my joy.

Rita is one of those rare individuals in the entertainment world who has a happy marriage. Over seven years ago Rita married a Baptist minister, and they have quite a unique ministry combining the two careers. In fact, the Rev. Norman Walter has played the part of the minister on *As the World Turns* since 1977. Recently his and Rita's characters were happily married on the show. They are now "Rev. and Mrs. Norm Frazier," and enjoy working together as husband and wife. Rita loves her new role as a pastor's wife now that her husband is pastoral counselor of the Calvary Chapel of Northern New Jersey. "I was made to be a part of a beautiful Christian fellowship like Calvary's, especially when Norm and I together can encourage good Christian marriages," Rita comments. She explains further:

> The thing in marriage that I think people have to realize is there is going to be brokenness in marriage. I always think of where the Lord has to remake that clay pot. He has to break us down to start over again. You can't get rid of the imperfections by just adding on; you've got to break down what is there already, especially when two people come together. They are pretty much set in their ways by the time they meet each other, and they've got to break old habits; and it hurts, and everything in us says no, you change—not me. And yet when we feel that brokenness and

we just want to crumble. That is really the feeling I've felt; and I just feel that the Lord has pruned me sometimes and it hurts so much. That is when two people are broken and they come together. It is the most incredible thing in the world. The Lord never takes away; He restores more than ever before. Christianity tells you that humility is the thing to strive for. This is what Norman and I both know. The first person to say I'm sorry, no matter whose fault it is, is the one God really blesses and encourages. This is what God wants for us. God will then lift us up, heal our hurts and bring us closer to Him and to each other. It's not a weakness to admit your faults.

Because of Jesus, I have an incredible, fantastic marriage. I never knew marriage could be this great. We are going to be celebrating our eighth year in December [1984] because God has told us to esteem each other greater than ourselves and to submit not only to each other but, of course, to His leadership. Without God, I am nothing; but with Jesus, because of Jesus, I am a somebody.

Bob Munger

6
Bob Munger

Bob Munger, the originator of *The Omen* film trilogy, was known a few years ago as the "whiz kid" of the advertising industry. Munger had managed to combine his flair for business, show-business creativity and deep religious beliefs into an incredibly successful career. While Munger directed his energy and creativity into the advertising profession, his interest in film remained.

Munger obtained his first insight into dramatic talent as a child and teen-age actor, working in countless television and radio shows as well as stage plays. His ability to speak well prepared him for the position he would later hold as the chairman of the Speakers' Bureau for the Western States Advertising Agencies Association.

Bob Munger was named to *Who's Who in California* years before he came to the film industry as a producer. The Freedom Foundation at Valley Forge awarded Munger its George Washington Honor Medal for his outstanding work on behalf of freedom in America. He was elected president of his college class of 4,000 and is chairman of the district scholarship committee for the University of Southern California.

The Omen, the biggest box-office success for 20th Century-Fox before *Star Wars,* was inspired when Munger realized that the conditions had been fulfilled for the coming of the

Celebrity Witness

Antichrist. *The Omen* introduced Damien Thorn, the Antichrist as a child. Two years later, in *Damien—Omen II*, the child had grown into an adolescent. In the release of *The Final Conflict*, Damien Thorn, 32, is the trusted advisor to the President of the United States. In his roles as the U.S. Ambassador to Great Britain and the president of the Thorn foundation, Damien amasses thousands of disciples and plunges the world into chaos.

> The book of Revelation tells us that the Beast of Satan will be a charismatic leader who will hold sway over the world before being destroyed by the Messiah. *The Final Conflict* resolves Damien's fate in accordance with this momentous prophecy.

How has success affected Munger's life?

> I've always been successful, but every now and then I've got to sit back and relax and say, "Wait a minute. I'm not doing it. The Lord is doing it." He is in control. I just kind of relax and see what happens, and amazing things do happen. I would say that my success has tended to hold me a bit in awe. Because the odds of anything as spectacular happening, like the things that have happened to me, are just mathematically way, way against you.

Most film makers face some opposition to their films. Surprisingly, Munger's opposition has tended to come from the church rather than from non-Christians.

> I think your greatest opposition comes from Christians. I don't get nearly as much trouble from Jews and atheists. If anything good is going to happen to advance the kingdom of the Lord in this world, you can be sure that the opposition will come from the church. It always has. Jesus Christ was certainly opposed, not by the heathen, but by the Pharisees.

Bob Munger

If Munger's criticism comes from the church, what do his colleagues from 20th Century-Fox feel about his Christian stand?

> Well, I don't really worry about it. I had one guy ask me if I wasn't a little bit embarrassed that sometimes someone might make fun of me. I said, "No." It is as if I went to some backward planet on my rocket ship and all the population gathered around me. They were laughing because they knew the only way to get somewhere was on a horse and buggy. Well, I wouldn't feel threatened by them and I wouldn't feel that I was better than they because I used to have a horse and buggy myself. I certainly wouldn't feel intimidated by them.

Does Munger feel that there will be more biblically based films in the future?

> I think there always have been many biblically based films. Now the problem you get is the distortion of the biblical message. There is a lot of that going on; and no matter what you do or what I try to do, somebody is going to say, "Well, that isn't my interpretation of the Bible." Well, you can't argue with that. Preachers argue about their interpretations, much less movie producers. But there are some gross distortions which I try to keep out of the pictures that I'm involved with, to the extent I can influence it.

In Munger's opinion, will Christian actors and actresses be having greater involvement in the feature film business?

> I certainly think so, but I would feel that every person is a candidate to be a Christian. I think, for example, one of the great opportunities to have more Christian actors and actresses is to convert some of the people that are already there. It is like

Celebrity Witness

this plan I heard about one time. They wanted only Christians in Congress, and they said, "We'll elect them all." Well, that would cost $300 million, I figured out. But for $10 million I could have two or three private missionaries to follow each Congressman around and get the ones that are already there saved. If your real goal is to have Christians in Congress, it would be much simpler to convert the ones that are already there. I'm talking about the matter of cost efficiency. If something costs $300 million to do one way and you are not even sure they'd all be elected—and how much time do you have to spend on the spiritual aspect of it if you are putting $300 million into the political aspect?

What future does Munger see for the film industry?

I think the film industry—the movie industry—is going to experience the greatest expansion it has ever had, probably by 600 percent in the next three to five years as a result of the video disk. This means that every home is going to be able to play movies for less than it costs you to go out and see them. You'll be able to play them over and over. Most people don't realize that the record business is about a $20 billion business and the film business is about a $3 billion business. I think those figures are going to flip-flop with the video disk. It would be as if you stood in front of a theater and it is $3 to get in, but it is $3.50 if you want to see it as well as hear it. I don't think they'd sell too many $3 tickets.

Does Munger think the media is the most effective way to witness today?

No. I think each person has got to seize the opportunities that he has every single day, whether it is the media or somewhere else. If you determine

Bob Munger

that God is only going to have you witness in a certain way, then you miss opportunities that come by. I don't think you can put God in a box by prescribing in advance what He is going to do in a certain way. I think this is a harmful way. It is important since we are approaching the end time of this world. We are going to be able to communicate Christ's message to every single solitary person in the world.

Susan Howard

7
Susan Howard

Susan Howard is known to television viewers all across America as the character of Donna Culver Krebbs on the top prime-time series, *Dallas*. Her career has gone through many highs and lows, but the show *Petrocelli* offered Susan her first major television role. Since then *Dallas* has offered her many more career opportunities. Susan comments on the events that have brought her to the prominent position she is in today:

> It really started after being a guest star on *Dallas*. I wasn't interested in getting involved in another series. It seemed very unfair that you could do this wonderful thing and they could cancel it. The second year on the show they wanted to try something. Would I do four episodes for them? I said, "Okay." At the end of that time, the network was interested enough in talking to Lorimar about adding my character to the show. They approached me about joining as a regular.

Susan was apprehensive about taking advantage of this opportunity, but decided to leave the decision in the Lord's hands.

Celebrity Witness

I thought, "Lord, what do You want me to do about this? You have opened all the doors. I did nothing to get this job. It was brought to me and laid in my lap. You offer me an opportunity to be in a show that looks like it is going to be a number one show with lots of visibility, with lots of opportunities to be seen and to be heard. Is that what You want me to do?" The answer kept coming up that that was the only door being opened to us. We didn't have an agent. We really wanted the Lord to bring in our lives what He wanted us to do. If we were to stay there, that's what would happen.

We said, "Okay." We know that gifts come from the Lord. Television is a business that you are involved in and you must take it that way. Never forget for a moment that you are in a business. You must approach it as such. We said, "All right, if we do make a commitment to the show, then there has to be a commitment coming back that you will agree to make the character one of the stars of the show." This would be full star billing. Pictures up and that kind of thing. Otherwise, we felt like it wasn't going to be right. The background was not exactly where the Lord was placing us. They agreed to it and we said, "All right." I went into it as a series regular.

Although Susan knows that she is where God wants her, there have been some trying times with her "star" status.

It hasn't been easy. It has been very difficult because it is such a popular show and there are so many people involved in it, so many egos involved in it, so much pressure from everything. There is a tendency, at times, to get caught up in it. You say, "Lord, you just aren't moving fast enough. Maybe I'd better help you. Maybe you just need a little help there, Lord." It's wonderful because that is when He

can begin to really teach you and deal with you. He is testing that faith that you've pronounced to have.
It just becomes so clear to me that for the first time in my life, I totally relied on Him for everything. The clothes that I would wear. The scripts that so distressed me at times. The character not being fulfilled as much as I would like it. It all was going to be taken care of because I had a promise from the Lord. I wasn't standing on it, I was doing it myself. I just really got to the point where I said, "Okay, I'm exhausted from it. I'm so tired. I'm so tired of wrestling with you. I'm tired of trying to take it away from you. I recognize that and forgive me. Forgive my greed and my lust and my ego and my pride and my haughty spirit and all of these things. Forgive me because I see them. I don't want them and if you want me to stay in this show, God, give me peace and grace about it, because I'm tired." I had the peace and the tranquility of really giving it over into His hands. And it will happen little by little, little by little. His timetable. It is so perfect because it happens when you are right with God.

Career strategy has changed quite a bit for Susan as she has allowed God to take over.

I never would do a talk show. I knew that this was such a big part of the business in order to have people know who you are. You do interviews, you do talk shows, you do photo layouts. That is part of the business that goes along with it. You put in and you get back—reciprocity.

I wasn't really putting anything into building a career other than going to work every day. That's not it. The Lord had to really teach me that. The Lord said, "Okay, what do you want, Susan?" I said, "Oh God, I want to work. I want to be able to do shows, to

Celebrity Witness

really have an opportunity. How do I do that?" He said, "You make a plan. You submit it to me and I will direct your path." I said, "Okay." He said, "Part of it is to do interviews, Susan. Don't you understand that in order to do the roles that you want to do, people have got to know who you are, my dear? Being a good actress on *Dallas* and having a community of peers respect you is wonderful, but it is not those people that hire you. Producers and directors and writers and advertising agencies and network executives hire you, and they want to hire nobility. The way you get that is you go on talk shows and you let people find out who you are. If you are afraid of people not liking you, maybe you don't like yourself enough. Maybe it is time you dealt with that area of your life." So we began to go through all of that.

I began to do talk shows. I was absolutely terrified! I found out that I had something to say and that people liked me and the things I always disliked about myself were things that bothered a lot of people. They had the same problems, sins, disappointments and aches as I did. But, we always want to appear perfect to people. They want, also, to know that you are a human being. The more that I'm doing of that, the more I can't begin to tell you, is coming back. The opportunities that are coming to me to want me to do other shows. It is exciting. It is all, really, because of obedience. It has nothing to do with anything other than obedience to the Lord.

Although Susan has an intensely personal relationship with Jesus now, it wasn't always that way. She talks about her understanding of Christianity as a child and during her young adult years.

I have known the Lord all of my life, really, since I was raised in a Christian home. I knew Him although

Susan Howard

I didn't know what He was about. I didn't have a personal walk with the Lord. I was baptized when I was nine years old—mainly because I was scared to death that I would go to hell. It didn't mean a thing to me other than that. I loved Jesus, but John 3:16 was Jesus. That was it. You didn't read the Word. You get it out at Christmastime, or whatever, and celebrate Christmas. Easter—and Easter eggs and all that kind of stuff. No one had ever told me about knowing the fullness of the Lord and participating in the kingdom that was here. I never knew about that. I never knew about the spirit of the Lord. I knew that you were saved—maybe. Because it all depended on how good you were. It was all boiled down to that. At the end of your life, if you were good enough, you might go to heaven. If you weren't there, there was a chance you might go to hell, so you really couldn't be too sure of your salvation. It was all up to you, every bit of it.

My husband, Calvin Chrane, was raised in a Christian home too. He went to church. Calvin knew more than I did. I think at one time, he even toyed with the idea of going into the ministry. When he was a young man, he always had that kind of faith. We were in Los Angeles and I would call myself a Christian if anyone ever asked me. Years before, I knew that the Bible was just really make-believe stories written to entertain you, to teach children how to not do certain things. I never questioned Jesus. It was the Old Testament stories.

Although Susan and her husband, Calvin, both considered themselves Christians, the emptiness in their lives caused them to seek for something more.

We had done *Petrocelli* and things were happening. We had a lot of things, but never enough.

Celebrity Witness

Our lives were very, very empty. Not as solid as it should be.

Calvin and I started talking. People would minister to you every now and then on the set. He said we needed to go to church. To go to church? Wow, that would be great. We hadn't been to church in so long. Okay, where will we go?

I remember passing a little church by the unemployment office. There was one right on the corner by where we lived, but that was not where we were to go. So, we went to the First Foursquare church in Van Nuys.

It was at this church service that Susan and Calvin found what they had been missing in their lives.

I don't remember exactly what Pastor Jack was talking about, but it had to have been a heart message about love and forgiveness, peace, emptiness and fulfillment in the Lord. I cried and cried during the whole service. My spirit was beginning to hear and it was just ministered to and stroked, as it were.

At the end of the service, he said, "If anyone would like to know more about walking with the Lord, one of our pastors will talk to you and show you a tape." A couple of weeks later, they said that they would like to pray for us. We went and they prayed for us. They said, "Do you need money, do you need healing, do you need this?" We said, "No, we just need Jesus." So right then and there, He just opened up His arms and we just jumped right into them and into the midst of the church.

We were baptized again because I said, "I know now what it means. I know what it is. I want to be baptized. I want to follow Jesus into those waters, because I know what it is all about. I want the fullness of the Holy Spirit. I want it all."

Susan Howard

> I think that is the only time the Lord said, "Okay, forget the patience. Here, you've got it all. Take it, my child. It is yours." From then on, it was as though I was taking one of these language classes where they teach you to speak the language very fast and you learn to really communicate in it. It is for businessmen who need to learn languages in six weeks. The Lord said, "You don't have time to fool around long because for what I have for you, you don't have time to be a baby for a very long period. I need you to move very fast in it." And we moved very fast in the Lord. I mean very fast, because we really asked for wisdom and we asked for patience and we asked for a little grace to be able to read and comprehend and to retain and just for His hand to always be there constantly pulling us back if we weren't on the right path as far as the books we were supposed to read, the classes we were supposed to go to and the people we were supposed to counsel with. It happened fast.
>
> Most things in my life, even career-wise, happened very slowly. It is wonderful, because there is a tendency to look around you and see how it is affecting everybody else and maybe get a balance in it. It happened very fast. He wanted it that way.

After Susan and her husband, Calvin, committed their lives to Jesus, they broke away from traditional agency representation and began to work together. Calvin comments on these changes:

> At the time we came to the Lord, our lives changed drastically, completely. All of a sudden, the Lord opened up doors, careerwise, for her and me. We had reached that point where the agency situation, the ones we were dealing with, were not comfortable at all. We just decided it was time to make a change,

Celebrity Witness

and so we released the agency we were with. Then we proceeded to start looking for new ones. Normally, you have one prepared, because you don't want this in-between sagging time.

The Lord just kind of held us in. He just said, "Hold off for a little bit." Before we knew it, we were so busy that we didn't have time to look and He was taking care of everything. We had no need for an agency. That has continued for four years. I must tell you, though, I'm always open and saying, "Lord, is it time? Is it time to bring another member into our organization?" We have grown now. I am beginning to feel that the Lord is giving me a release now. Maybe it is time to do something like that. I don't know for sure. I am just open to that.

We work together. We don't always agree. There is no question about that. The thing that makes it work is that we both listen to what each has to say. By doing that, we kind of get a balance. We come to an agreement, and whatever that decision is, we both give place to that wholeheartedly with the understanding that it is the right one. That is what the Lord means it to be. It just takes care of itself. Sometimes it is not an easy decision to come to either. We go through many things before we come to an agreement. We just listen to each other and to the Lord, first of all. Praise God, it seems to have worked well.

It is getting to a point again that He is taking us another step. Time-wise I don't have the time to do the things as an agent. Maybe we'll need to hire somebody. We have a specific goal of producing some films together—Susan and I. Each of us has worked on different projects—never together. We are searching for a story, searching for a script right now.

Susan Howard

As the Lord has brought Susan and Calvin to positions of prominence, they have found new opportunities for ministry. Susan talks about the ministry she feels that the Lord has given her.

> My ministry is to be able to see what is happening in the lives of those that I work with. I then pray about it in my own devotional time. I have talked to people who think they've made it, who think they know it all, and if they are already caught up in a science-of-mind religion, a cultish type of thing, you are not going to change them by your talk. You are going to have to live your life out, and you are going to have to pray a lot for the Lord to give you entry into that. Otherwise, you will be very destructive and you will be of no value to Him whatsoever. The biggest ministry that I have is in these things because I travel a lot and I talk to a lot of newspapers. It is more to the people at large who say, "She is successful and she is saying that Jesus Christ is Lord of her life and that every phase of her life He has kingship over."

Susan found the need to enlarge her circle of friends as she began to reach others in ministry.

> When I first came to church, I would congregate with only the actors and actresses because they were the ones who could understand my problems. I began to realize that it was more important that I fellowship with people who had a knowledge of it, yes, that's important, but who maybe are not actors or performers because I needed these other people, their special way of praying and anointing that was speaking through them.

Susan has found that her greatest influence is with the young people that make up her audience.

Celebrity Witness

I know what the Lord is using me for—kids. It is a big responsibility to be where I am right now. You cannot just have a kid come up to you and ask you for an autograph and just shove them aside because you are so tired and don't have time for them. Jesus had time for everybody, and He had to have been exhausted by the end of His day, and still He would go and pray to His Father. The reality and the depth of that began to hit me. There are times when I got off the plane and the first thing they do is shove a camera in my face. I really just want to sleep or say something, but I can't because that was not the witness that was given to me. If we are going to be the image and the likeness of the Father, of Jesus. Let Him work His life through you, and He will give you the strength. Then go to the hotel and collapse and tell them, "In twelve hours I will come out again." But take the sabbath and rest. Learn your authority in the Lord, but also at the same time remember that sometimes you are going to be caught off guard or out of where you thought you were ready. In that instance, you really have to rely on the peace of the Lord to be with you. To minister to those children or to those adults when all they want to do is to touch you.

These are ministering hands. What are you going to do? Reach out to somebody and shove them out of the way? You can't do that. You don't have the right to do that as a Christian. Other people can do it, but I cannot do that.

I had a man come and build shutters for my living room. He was a Christian. He was talking to Calvin and said, "You know, it is different being a Christian in a job, because you can't just leave it if something is wrong. If it is a warped piece of shutter, you've got to replace it, because people look at your work and

Susan Howard

say, "Christian! Would you look at this thing!" It is an incredible responsibility to people. My heart goes out to them. The sick and the dying and the lost and the spiritually hungry in the world. It is the depth of compassion you need to have for them. It isn't an easy thing to do and I'm not always successful at it. Reaching toward that mark of the high calling of God in Christ Jesus. Hallelujah!

Criticism from other Christians is a frequent problem that is dealt with by those in the entertainment profession. Fortunately Susan hasn't had to deal with an excessive amount of judgment.

I have never felt that kind of yoke of criticism from my brothers and sisters. I think it is because of the mature believers that I have for a long time moved in the midst of. I'm sure it exists. Maybe the Lord has just shielded me. I don't need that. I've had it asked of me by Christians how I could do a show like *Dallas.* I don't worry about answering it anymore. I'm where I should be. I have peace within. Sometime maybe God can answer that for you. If you really want to know, ask Jesus. If you'll really knock, He'll tell you why I am where I am.

Right now I feel that I'm in the center of His will. He showed me how it felt to be out of it, to be moving along the path that you knew, looking straight ahead into the eyes of Jesus and you see the cows grazing in the pasture. All of a sudden, there is a head-on collision with something you didn't expect. Good. Go through those trials and tribulations. Wonderful. Take a little detour off over there and learn a little bit more. Because just when you think you know it all, He says, "Now it is time to move on up to another step." You say, "Oh, Lord, I've been going along for such a nice clip here. I've been good about praying

Celebrity Witness

for other people, my country, my president and my pastor and missionaries." It's really important to get down there early in the day and seek the Lord. When do you really submit yourself and say, "Okay, I'm ready for you to show me more things about myself?" That is what He has been doing this year.

Insecurity tends to mark actresses and actors. Susan talks about this attitude in her profession.

> The majority of actors and actresses are very insecure human beings. This is because your life style is based on what somebody else judges you to be. You are either too fat for this role or too thin, too tall, too old, you're white or black or green or yellow or whatever it happens to be. You are constantly up for grabs, as it were, to somebody else's opinion. You are dealing with a very frightful, delicate group of people. Then, when they make it, they tend to be absolute monsters because they throw back what they were given. The Lord says that too. Whatever you give out, so much of it is going to come back. You understand why a lot of people do become monsters, because they have been given nothing but rejection and then they make it—this obscure person that nobody ever really thought would make it, makes it. And, unfortunately, that is what happens. You read more about that than you do about the good guy that makes it. You are never going to combat that in this world.

Susan shares what she finds to be the most difficult thing being in the public eye:

> The most difficult thing is committing to it. Of really using what the Lord has given me. I really just had a hard time. I thought, "I'm an artist, and an artist just doesn't go out and do these kinds of things,

Susan Howard

Lord." I just don't do that because I'm a loner. I am a very private, shy person who really doesn't want people to get that close. "Don't get that close to me because I might have to tell you about me. I might have to share something and then you'll know." That has been the hardest thing—being open. I don't have trouble meeting people, because I like people, but I have a difficulty in wanting to get on a one-to-one basis with them.

They know in my resumé that I am a Christian. What are they going to say to me? What am I going to say? He says, "Don't worry about it. I've told you not to plan what you are going to say, because when you need the words I'll give them to you." I get to the point where I can really go in and enjoy them. Sometimes I never mention it and they never bring it up. I talk about whatever it happens to be. There are other times when I'm right there for that person at that time, and the Lord really wanted to reach out and touch that person. I've had people cry on interviews with me before. I've never had anyone pray for salvation, but I've had a deep discussion about their walk and belief and they ask me questions about all the science mind stuff. You really have an opportunity.

You can't be stupid. You must read these things. A lot of Christians say, "I can't read that stuff." If the Lord has given you a platform from which to speak and you are constantly coming up against people, in front of people who have deep, honestly motivated questions, are you going to answer them in ignorance? I didn't say study them or practice them, but at least know what it is that you are dealing with. Understand the spirit that is there.

Read some of the books of these people who have come out from under the cults, who have been in the

Celebrity Witness

> midst of them. Understand what humanism is about. How can you intellectually discuss anything with anybody if you don't understand where they are coming from? You don't have to be afraid—you are under the covering of the only thing in the whole wide world that matters. You might be the only person that they will ever come face to face with that can have an intelligent discussion about it with them. I don't know all of it, because I haven't read all of it, but I know enough of some of it, and the Lord has sent some of those people.
>
> I believe most Christians don't do it because they think somehow that they are going to be tainted by it. "I know that it will rub off on me, it will rub right off. I can catch it like a cold. Sin—I'm going to catch it."

Susan ends her comments by giving advice to those who are aspiring to positions of stardom.

> I would say not to go after stardom, because that is not what I ever went after. I think that is one of the things that I've never had to battle—wanting to be a moneyed whatever. I did have to come face to face with—yes, I did want to become a star. I wanted the recognition that went along with it. My pursuit was to be considered an actress. That's what I coveted. That's what I lusted after—to be Ingrid Bergman. Somebody that was considered credible. That was my biggest bondage.
>
> I would say to someone who wants it, "If the Lord has given you that in your heart, then pursue it. He will cause things to happen as a result of your obedience to Him. All good things come from the Lord anyway. I would encourage them because we need Christians in our business. We need actors, writers and directors and producers to move into it.

Susan Howard

The doors are open. I believe that people get to a point where they have seen so much garbage in their lives and scripts that come across their desk and they are so despondent and depressing. They have produced so much garbage and directed so much that when light walks in, whether they follow it or not, they would like to be around it because it makes them feel better. I believe that the doors are open.

Joan Winmill Brown

8
Joan Winmill Brown

Joan Winmill Brown was an established British actress when she came to the United States several years ago. She has had numerous film roles in America as well as in England. Major U.S. films have included *Time to Run,* and *No Longer Alone,* her autobiography. Joan is married to Bill Brown, president of World Wide Pictures.

According to Joan, what place do Christian actors and actresses hold in the feature film business?

> I'm praying that because of the election, there will be a surging toward good family films—films that Christian actors and actresses could feel they could be in without compromising their stand. When I first came to the Lord, it was very hard to find those. I used to compromise in my thinking. One film, *The Little Hut,* that would get a G rating today was considered quite risqué then. I hadn't grown enough in the Lord to realize that He was going to take care of me, and I just felt I had to take this because I didn't have too much money in the bank. I took it; and as soon as I took it and signed the contract, I knew I'd done the wrong thing. The Lord taught me so many things through that. I feel that actors and actresses —anyone in the media—have such a responsibility

to portray the right kind of role because their influence is so tremendous.

Would Joan play an immoral person in a film if the film made a point?

> It is hard to say. I'd have to look at the whole script. I think you can get across to the public these roles without going to the depths—swearing and anything like that.

Joan further describes this dilemma:

> I went to a movie a few years ago, and I was just shocked. If you keep going, you may say it is terrible, terrible, but then it doesn't shock you. I think that is very dangerous—to realize that we can compromise so easily.

Does Joan think that Christian actors and actresses are hard to find?

> I think more and more we are going to see them coming forward. It is very hard to live in Hollywood with the decadence on the sets. It is just wild. Christians need to be actors and actresses. Because our very nature is very vulnerable, very sensitive, the actors and actresses can easily be overwhelmed.

Joan explains that her husband is working towards films and movies to be shown on network television.

> This goal is one of the visions that the Lord has given us—to get this stuff in and take our inheritance. God has given us the cattle on 1,000 hills and that includes the airways.

How would Joan like other Christians to pray for her and her husband?

> We should pray that the Lord will really guide us,

especially my husband. The biggest problem is finding Christian writers. Pray for our being kept as close to the consciousness of Christ as possible. It is easy to think if we did this, we would get more (clients) people. People come because of what the company represents. People come with a hunger in their hearts. We ask the Lord to give us a zealous attitude, but one that will not offend people.

Part II

Celebrities in the Music Industry

Jeannie C. Riley

9
Jeannie C. Riley

Jeannie C. Riley was truly an overnight success in the music world with the release of her hit song, "Harper Valley PTA" in 1968. One week Jeannie was a secretary, the next week she was the singer of a recording that had sold a million copies. Although more than fifteen years have passed, Jeannie's fame has continued to endure. Jeannie comments on how her interest in country music began at an early age.

As a fan of the entertainment business when I was growing up, I could watch a country music show and hear them call someone's name on the stage, all bright and sparkly, and I would think, "Oh, how exciting, how glamorous—what it must be like!" I would have to say that there was so much of that vanity stuff—folly ideas—that drove me to choosing my life's work. It should have been because of the music, because it was a gift that God had given me that I wanted to share with others. There was a certain element of that. But, I have to admit, it was more vanity than anything else, more of the selfish idea—"I want to get famous, I want to get rich. This will be my vehicle to carry me there." I think that's a trap for anybody, because when anything becomes a daily routine, commonplace, if it's not based on the rock of a true godly ambition, it's not going to hold up anyway. Then I began to ask myself, years after being in the business, "How did I get here?" I don't think I had a single-minded ambition toward the music of it to bring it to pass, but there was a certain energy.

Jeannie believed in her dream, and this faith eventually brought about the success she was seeking.

>I wouldn't even hang curtains in our little quaint apartment for a year or two before I recorded "Harper Valley." I would put off some certain work like waxing the floors that would last, maybe, a couple of weeks, for, why should I do this today because it may be tomorrow when my break comes? And I lived daily, expectantly. If I went to the mailbox, my break may be in the mailbox. Somebody knocked at the door and my heart would leap. There comes my break. Somebody's coming after me as if success was going to track me down and land in my lap. And you know what? When it did come, it wasn't any of my own pursuit. I didn't pursue it, but when it came, it literally tracked me down and jumped in my lap.
>I was talked into recording "Harper Valley PTA." My arm was just about twisted by friends to do it. A best friend of mine had a husband who wrote for Shelby Singleton who had Plantation Records. He heard "Harper Valley" as a demo by someone else. Loved the song, but was not interested in the singer. He heard a tape of me that I had done on some of my friend's songs. He said, "Go get her. I've got the song and we will make history. We'll cut a number one record." And we did—a multimillion seller—after a week of my friends laboring over the idea that I must do this, that this was my break. And I thought,

Jeannie C. Riley

> Well, no. It's not RCA, it's not Columbia, it's not Capitol or any of the majors that I wanted to hold out for. Who was Shelby Singleton and what was Plantation Records? I did not want to do it, but I was talked into it. It became my break. It literally did track me down that way. I don't take credit for that saying, "I brought that to pass." But it is a godly principle. Even though I wasn't godly, He still honors His principles.

Jeannie's fame brought about a tremendous change in her life style that affected her family and friends and added stress to her marriage. This stress led to her divorce from her husband, Mickey, whom she remarried in 1975. Jeannie comments on a few of these changes.

> My life style changed completely. I didn't hoard much up, I was generous with myself and everybody else, too. It was a presumptuous thing. I thought the flow has started and it's never-ending. It wasn't that I thought I was so talented it had to keep on. Somehow or other, even before I knew Christ, I knew I was just blessed with a fabulous opportunity through that song, and yet I wasn't a good steward of all that "Harper Valley" provided me with—in the way of money or time well-spent. My choices were not what they should have been. But all those things were a learning process to me.

Jeannie's success also brought a few problems into her life. She talks about the thing that has been the most difficult for her to deal with.

> Probably, struggling with the image created by the very song that gained me the popularity with the people. The image was one of sassiness and the old finger pointing image, looking like, "Approach me and I'll hit you." People were entertained by the song

and, perhaps the entertainer, but they did not feel close to me. I wanted so much to be loved. I wanted to be the girl next door. People expected me to be in my little miniskirts and boots with my cleavage showing all the time. This is stuff to alienate women and to have men think of you only in terms that you wouldn't prefer that they did. Even then, I didn't want that kind of image, but I was helpless to do anything about it. I believed whoever was in charge. They said that I must always be in my "Harper Valley" rig—to maintain that image. Just because they said so, I thought it was the final word. If only I had known the Lord then and been as insistent on keeping His Word as I was on keeping the producer's words, and my manager's words in those early days. There's no telling what I would have accomplished with the Lord.

I was so moldable that I had very little creative input in anything that I did. It was frustrating to me. But, through Christ, the struggle with my image ended long ago. Every interview that I used to do would read something like "Singer Fights Image," or something like that. God is our defense and we don't have to spend time defending ourselves, because it makes other people defensive. The public had accepted me in that role, and then fighting it was like a slap in the face to the very people who helped me to achieve it. They were offended, I think, with the idea "She's biting the hand that feeds her. Is she saying we were wrong? We like that image. Now, she's telling us we were wrong to accept it?"

When Jeannie became a Christian, she found herself caught between the secular and Christian world. She found it difficult to fit in anywhere.

Jeannie C. Riley

> I can understand the public and don't blame them. But it was very hard becoming a Christian in show business, with an already established image which was derogatory to the things I now represent. There had to be a visible change. People are threatened by that kind of change. Christianity represents such a sacrifice to them. It's going to cost somebody something. That's all they seem to think about.
>
> There are other people that rise up in show business to a measure of fame and give God the credit all the way up. People are not threatened by that. They didn't know that person by any other image. They didn't want to accept a different me, and I can understand, from the flesh, their attitude. But nevertheless, I had to live in it and it's difficult in show business. It was difficult as far as advertising went. When I got in the Christian marketplace I was still in the secular field, professionally. The Lord's kept that door open for me and used me to carry His message to what seems to be an almost foreign mission field. Entertainment is a foreign mission field for the gospel. Are people coming to see the Christian entertainer or are they coming to see the secular performer?

Jeannie has found that her greatest criticism has come from the Christian community, not from non-Christians.

> I've had to qualify it a few times—how I can be a Christian and still be in a secular field of music. I don't know why it's so frowned upon by so many people in the body. Now, your condemnation doesn't come from people outside the body. Not at all from the ones you'd hope to win. It comes from your brothers and sisters in Christ that have a limited vision for what God can do. You know, if a person is in real estate when they accept Christ, nobody

Celebrity Witness

thinks it's odd if they continue to sell property that may become this or that. In other words, the real estate agent is not responsible for what the people are going to do with that property. They don't sell just to Christians and they don't sell just to churches to build churches on. They remain in a professional, secular business. They remain in that kind of business, but people don't think anything about it. I think a good example is a truck driver. What if we expected every truck driver that got saved to quit driving for the company he's driving for and started driving only chapel buses around the country? Where is our food going to come from? Where are our clothes going to come from? But nobody condemns the truck driver for continuing to drive his truck. But in entertainment, more than any other business, there's this thing that if you've become a Christian, why didn't you drop every single, solitary secular song that you sing and sing only gospel? I won't sing something unscriptural, but that doesn't mean that I have to sing all Scripture.

Jeannie closes her comments by giving advice to those who are seeking fulfillment through the stardom that Nashville offers.

Gifts of life may be nice—they are—but they're enjoyable for such a short season, without fellowship with the giver. If you're looking for things in life as a means to happiness, you're just not going to find it. Only as we have our priorities lined up correctly, can we properly enjoy this life. Putting God first, we can enjoy the things He provides, but I maintain that we should seek first the kingdom of God and His righteousness and He'll bring all these other things to pass.

Trumpeter Johnny Zell with Lawrence Welk

10
Johnny Zell

Johnny Zell, trumpeter on *The Lawrence Welk Show,* began his career as an Army corporal stationed in Colorado Springs, Colorado. Zell was chosen by the North American Air Defense Command to represent them by doing a guest appearance on *The Lawrence Welk Show.* Twelve months later, when his stint in the Army was up, Zell became a regular on the show.

At a point of deep need in Zell's life, Tom Netherton, vocalist on the show, joined the orchestra for a rehearsal. Zell was experiencing a personal tragedy and Netherton sensed Zell's need. Zell explains:

> I noticed a look in his eyes one day and I went up to him and I said, "Tom, you really have a great look on your face. What makes you so happy?"

Netherton told Zell that he had accepted the Lord seven years previously. He gave Zell a *Living Bible* and suggested that he read the Gospel of John.

> So I read the Gospel of John all the way through, and I gave it back to him and said, "Tom, it is wonderful. It looks really great, but I'm not ready for this type of thing right now. I can't believe all those miracles and all this." Tom looked at me and said, "Why don't you read it again?" So I did. I took it home

Celebrity Witness

and I read it all through again and I knew that what was being said was wonderful, but I didn't want to make a decision for something like that unless it was really a true decision and something that would really be concrete. So I took it back to Tom and told him my predicament. Well, he had confidence in his product because he said to me, "Read it again." So I read it again and I got to the third chapter where Nicodemus came to Jesus by night. Jesus told him he must be born again. It was like the words just lifted right off the page at me. It wasn't "Nicodemus, you must be born again." I was in a hotel room on the road with the Welk show. We were in Montreal, Quebec, and I got down on my hands and knees and I said, "Lord, if these things are really true, if this is really you and you are here with me in this room, I really need you in my life." The most beautiful peace and calm came upon me that I've ever known, and from that moment on my whole life has turned completely around.

How has Zell's celebrity status affected his spiritual life?

Staying in the Word is like having your spiritual cup of coffee in the morning. It primes you for the day. It primes you for the problems of the day. It gives you the wisdom and understanding you need for the day. I used to worry about things that were going to happen in a week. The Lord is taking that out of me and I'm going moment by moment. I'm able to relax so much more.

Because of it, I like to read early in the morning and get that spiritual cup of coffee for about an hour. Also, I have a study guide. I get in the habit and routine of reading that, and after I've read that particular portion, I pick a spot in the Bible myself and maybe read a couple of verses there. I

Johnny Zell

find out more often than not that they correlate and complement each other.

Soon after becoming a Christian, Zell met his wife-to-be, Laura. After a four-year courtship, the Zells married. Zell comments on his views of marriage.

> We've learned together that marriage is most important in life. It is above your work or anything because of the marriage of the body of Christ and the church. I am the head of the wife and the wife is to be submissive to me, because that is what the Lord says. I don't understand why that is, but that is the way it is; so I'm going to treat it that way and so is Laura. We figure from what the Word says, that the marriage is a witness of that. Christ gave us the Holy Spirit as an engagement ring. We are all going to be together in heaven. So our marriage is a picture of that and it is held very sacred to us. We'd get out of the music business in a minute if it was affecting our marriage.

How does Zell want other Christians to pray for him?

> I would want them to pray for me to be unselfish, more unselfish than I've ever been and to be very content with exactly what I'm doing, because if you are not content, you are going to be grabbing for other things. Unfortunately, this music business breeds that kind of thought. Because you are never quite happy with what you've got—you grab a little more of this. It is very hard. The glamour is 1 percent. It is 99 percent hard work.
>
> I would pray for contentment. People say, "I wish I could do that." Walk a mile in somebody else's shoes and you'll be glad you're in your own; if you are in the will of God and if you are reading His Word and He is speaking to you. Not that you should be content not

Celebrity Witness

to do anything else, but be content while you are there. We can all identify with pride, and it sneaks up on you at the worst possible moment.

What has Zell found to be the hardest thing to cope with as a Christian in the entertainment world?

> We've had problems, but the Lord has been so gracious. We've read in the Psalms to wait on the Lord. Like Psalm 30 says, even when your enemy is trying to snare you, the Lord is in complete charge. He loves us so much and no matter what happens, it is in His plan unless you've fallen into some sin. That word *practice* is so important because you can fall from time to time. That is not the big deal. It is when you've got a sin that you are practicing and staying in. As far as coping, just trusting Him and knowing Him better, seems to make the problems not stay around long.

Why does Zell think that the world is more open than other Christians?

> A lot of brothers and sisters really love the Lord, and they get into His Word and maybe they get a triumph over a weakness in their lives. Such victory can cause pride. Because they've had a triumph over it, they may lord it over you. I remember when the Lord took smoking away from me. I had a tendency to look at other smokers and say what a terrible thing they were doing. I was just being prideful because I thought I'd taken it away from myself, and here the Lord had done everything.

Johnny is enthusiastic about his spiritual life now.

> Being a Christian is so wonderful, because you can live such a joyous life, go to sleep with peace in your heart and wake up each morning ready to

Johnny Zell

go . . . . The Word means so much to me. I know that the more I stay in the Bible and read it, the more God tells me that He loves me through it and the more I'll be able to act in the power of the Holy Spirit.

According to Webster's dictionary, a trumpeter is "a trumpet player" and "one that praises or advocates." Johnny Zell fits into both categories since receiving Jesus as Lord and Savior. Zell wants his trumpet to be an instrument of joy. He is aware that in the Old Testament the trumpet, or shofar, was a necessary worship instrument used in the Temple to bring the people into remembrance before the Lord (Lev. 25:9). Zell also realizes that a trumpet will announce the Second Coming of Christ.

In conclusion, Johnny states:

None of the life on the other side of the cross can compare to the new life I know in Jesus Christ today! Now I can serve the Lord playing trumpets, giving back to Him talents He's given to me. I think that's the main thing in my life from now on.

Noel Paul Stookey

11
Noel Paul Stookey and Karla Sarro

Noel Paul Stookey, former member of the popular folk group in the '60's, "Peter, Paul and Mary," leads a vastly different life today from when he was on the road touring with the group.

In 1968, shortly before the group disbanded, the trio performed a concert in Austin, Texas. Backstage, Paul met a young man who introduced him to Jesus Christ. This served to be a major turning point in Paul's life. When he accepted Christ's lordship in his life, Paul began to use his given name, Noel.

After his conversion, Noel realized his main ministry was to his family. Family became his top priority instead of making money. Stookey moved his family from suburban New York to South Blue Hill, Maine. He bought an abandoned four-story henhouse and twenty-seven acres of land. In this renovated henhouse, Stookey established a recording/animation complex known as "Neworld Media." This studio caters to artists and musicians who wish to create free from city distractions.

Stookey's work at the studio has expanded. From what started out as a personal recording studio for Noel to complete his contract with Warner Brothers, it has expanded to house his own record company (Neworld Records) where he has produced his own albums for national distribution.

Celebrity Witness

Stookey has also produced a children's radio program, *Sandman,* at his studios. Stookey now travels on a limited basis with his group Bodyworks, featuring vocalist, Karla Sarro.

Did other entertainers accept Noel when he made his commitment to Christ?

> No, I don't think so, but eventually they have to. They have to. They didn't take me seriously. I think conditionally they kept waiting for me to "come off it."

Stookey talks about his relationship with Bob Dylan.

> He witnessed to me more than I witnessed to him. Initially, fourteen years ago, he was instrumental in my using the Bible as research material. Of course, the earnest desire to have a full and meaningful life leads to only one place, and that is standing in front of the throne. Fortunately, Bob was there when I needed somebody to show me how to take that last step.

These days, Noel limits his performances to about eighty per year, with possible overseas tours when he can take his family. Has he had any problems dealing with other Christians while he has been a celebrity?

> No, I haven't. I retired in 1970 and worked sporadically until 1978. I really work on a limited basis now; so when I do work, it's primarily to evangelize one way or the other.

Noel doesn't think his concerts are overly evangelistic.

> I feel that the testimony is in song. For instance, I think "Miracles" is a very heady kind of tune intellectually. It pinpoints an understanding of coincidence. You can isolate the means of a miracle;

Noel Paul Stookey and Karla Sarro

> you can describe the way in which a miracle was done, but that never detracts from the miracle. Before I was a Christian, I performed to entertain and be entertained. I derived a lot of satisfaction from performing. I still do! But now the satisfaction is similar to that which you get from doing a favor or a kindness for someone. I feel that I'm of service to the people in my audience. I feel that I am of use to somebody out there, either intellectually or because I'm touching an area that they've thought about. Or maybe I have attacked directly a problem that they have been up against and they need to know that somebody else has had that same problem and overcame it.

What does Noel find to be his main problem being in the public eye and maintaining a Christian witness?

> Boldness. It is being secure in the fact that you are being led of the Spirit to say something rather than striving to place God in a situation. Because if you do that, then it is not anointed. Unless it is strictly scriptural, it is probably going to return void.

How does Karla think pride affects a performer?

> That is my biggest enemy—ego. It is to me the devil. The devil uses ego, and that is what we all struggle to crucify.

Karla talks about her working relationship with Noel.

> It is a pleasure to work with Noel, because if it wasn't for Noel, I wouldn't get to meet all those famous people. I always wondered what it would be like. Because I'm shy, I overextended myself in the other direction, so my shyness won't show. I think we are all a little awed by the people we see on the silver screen. We just can't help that. It is human. We

Celebrity Witness

go through situations that make me realize that they are just people.

It isn't easy and most of the time they aren't anything like their image. It's like you meet a guy and you think this guy is really macho, and the guy turns out to be a little Caspar Milquetoast. It is his character you are relating to. If the Lord should ever put me in a position of renown, I wouldn't want to be stereotyped. It is limiting.

Karla describes how she met the Lord.

I always sought the truth of God. I'd always read. I'd always believed in the Creator. I started working with Noel. I'd always had a feel for gospel music. I did not want to be a Christian. I felt that Christians were nowhere. I just didn't commit myself to anything.

The minute it was put to me through Noel and with the little seeds that had been planted along the way, I finally made the connection that Jesus was saying, "I Am." Then I started looking in the New Testament. I knew something was happening to me. I was on the road. I knew I had to make a decision. I repented and asked Him to come in. He zapped me with the Holy Spirit.

Karla's dedication to the Lord is now similar to that of Noel's. Together with the band, Bodyworks, they are able to share their belief that Jesus Christ is the only unchanging answer for the problems of mankind.

Danniebelle Hall

12
Danniebelle Hall

Danniebelle Hall was originally from Pittsburgh, Pennsylvania. She says her family was financially poor but spiritually rich. Danniebelle gave her life to the Lord at the age of twelve. She went on to be an active church participant, choir leader and pianist. Contented with playing the piano, Danniebelle did not begin to sing until she was nineteen or twenty. In the mid-1960's Danniebelle formed a gospel music quartet, "The Danniebelles." The group toured with Stanley Mooneyham, several Billy Graham crusades and with the U.S.O. The group split up in the early 1970's. Danniebelle later sang with Andrae Crouch and went on her own in 1977.

Danniebelle describes her beginning.

> I began recording ten years ago when I had my group "The Danniebelles." We made an album which couldn't go very far because it was not distributed properly. You can't do much with an unknown company. It is fine with an unknown company if they have the distribution ability. If they can distribute your album and get it into the marketplace, fine.

What events led to Danniebelle's association with Andrae Crouch?

Celebrity Witness

> Andrae just asked me to join the group. I started hanging around and I sang with him for about four years. I sang at the Christian Booksellers' Convention in 1973. At the convention there were several record companies, and they expressed an interest in me. Before that time I was almost begging people—you know, knocking on doors, that kind of thing—for a recording contract. The Lord opened up the door at that convention. Several companies were asking me. I signed with Light Records. Three or four years after that I went on with Sparrow, and now I'm on Onyx Records, which is a subsidiary of the Benson Company.

When Danniebelle went with Andrae Crouch and the Disciples, she was already established as a singer.

> It was just the two ministries merging. Of course, his ministry was a lot more recognized by the public. Mine was just as viable a ministry in my mind and spirit as his was. It was just that I wasn't as well-known and I know that being with him opened a lot of doors for me. It is just like I believe the Lord allowed me to come into that position so I could meet people and also be a help to his ministry. I feel that I served my purpose in the time we were together. Then it was the time for me to move on and also help other young artists doing the same kind of thing.
>
> When I say "young," I mean new in the business of recording and singing. I wanted to be helpful to them in any way that I could. I believe that is really why the Lord had me there with Andrae—so I could help his ministry and so I could learn a lot of things and so I could pass on the favors to somebody else.

Why did Danniebelle leave the group and go out on her own?

Danniebelle Hall

> When I recognized that the Lord had given me a ministry, I really wanted to be sensitive to the Lord and His timing as to when I should move into the solo ministry. There was a time I had been anxious about it, but the Lord just allowed me to rest in Him and to relax and know that in His own timing it would come about. It was as I became comfortable where I was that the Lord opened up another door for me.

Danniebelle talks about how traveling has affected her family life.

> I think unless you are traveling together—husband and wife, or kids—I think you are going to run into problems. Even then, when people travel together, they run into problems. When you have one staying home and the other leaving, there are bound to be problems that have to be worked out. I'm finding that the Lord can work those problems out, although not always the way you think they should be worked out.

Danniebelle continues her comments on this subject.

> It is a Bible principle that people do not go out by themselves. I traveled for three years by myself, and Dora Taylor has been traveling with me since then. She has a ministry of her own; but she has been helping me in mine and, of course, that makes her just as much a part of my ministry. It is a real credit to her that she would subject herself to my ministry. She certainly has been a blessing to me.

What problems does Danniebelle have to face being in the public eye? Adulation?

> That is true. I don't think it is so much a problem as it is an attitude you have to deal with, an attitude of your heart. You have to really develop the proper

Celebrity Witness

attitude toward what you are doing. I think sometimes, speaking for myself, I tend to forget why the Lord has me out; and that is usually when the Lord puts me in a very humbling experience to remind me of why I'm there. Believe me, I've been in several instances where the Lord has brought me to a place of humility and complete dependence on Him. You'd never be able to stand the situation, but knowing the Lord is leading and guiding you, you can endure anything. In many cases it becomes enjoyable.

What does Danniebelle think about the problem of pride that most entertainers have to deal with?

That was the first thing the Lord hated. He goes to any lengths to eradicate pride in the believer. Often that means you have to be reduced to nothing, be brought to a place of total dependence upon the Lord before you realize that this is the way the Lord wants you. When people put you up, emulate you, you realize what a tremendous responsibility you have. I almost feel like being responsible for people when, in reality, the Lord is responsible for them. What you are responsible for is to be faithful to the Lord. He is always faithful to us. I used to feel a tremendous responsibility that there were certain things that I couldn't do or say. I felt very bound because I was in this position. What if people see me doing this or that? Of course, I use discretion in anything I do. God tells us in all things to be moderate and temperate. I've learned a new liberty in Christ that I can be myself, because I've settled the fact that the Lord works through me and that His anointing abides and rests on my life and that I can literally call down the anointing of God for that specific time and in whatever I'm doing. When I'm finished, I'm still Danniebelle—a human person.

Danniebelle Hall

I think a lot of times people go off on a tangent and they think they are always that person who is up front, always that one who is ministering. Satan takes advantage of those times when the applauding is over and the curtain is down. Those are usually the most lonely times. That is when you become the most vulnerable to an attack from Satan. He puts everything in your way right then and there. I find that is the time you must be rooted and grounded in the Word. You must have the understanding that the Lord is using you, not because of yourself, but in spite of yourself.

How would Danniebelle like other Christians to pray for her?

I would ask them to pray that I'd continue to be sensitive to the voice of the Lord and understand what His will for my life is. I realize that it may mean that I'd be in a changing situation and that I'd have to change and be flexible wherever He'd decide to use me. That would be my desire—to be sensitive. I'd like to be like a finely tuned instrument that the Lord can just choose to play at any time, that I'd be in tune whenever He decides to use me. Sometimes we can get out of tune with what the Lord is doing. We can get out of touch with ourselves. We can get out of touch with what is going on in the world so we really are of no value. It is like a rusty tool the Lord has to clean up so He can use it. I'd like to be that finely tuned, well-oiled instrument that He can use.

What does Danniebelle see in the future for her life?

I see expansions into other aspects of the ministry. I see that I'm going to be involved in the business part of the ministry a lot more than I am right now, producing new records under different artists. I'm writing a book. I've been working on it for the past two or three years. I'd like to get that published, record more, begin my own publishing company and that sort of thing. I want to involve myself in a lot of business aspects. Because I just feel that Christian artists need Christian business people to turn to for help and advice, for backing and that sort of thing. I feel that when you invest in a Christian artist, you are investing in the Kingdom.

Reba Rambo

(Photo courtesy of John Loizides.)

13
Reba Rambo

Reba Rambo is an established singer and composer in Christian music circles. Until seven years ago, Reba used to sing with her mother and father with "The Rambos." Since branching off on her own, Reba has found many more opportunities open to her.

Reba talks about her background.

> My mother started traveling by herself when she was twelve. She had a little name tag around her neck. Her mother would put her on the bus, and the minister in the city where she was going would pick her up at the bus station. Dad met mother at one of the church services where she sang.
>
> They were married—and about eighteen months later, I was born. So I've always been around singers. My parents were evangelists. They worked little churches. We had an old car with slick tires, the whole bit. It was not the glamorous singing life at all. It was the very poor evangelistic side of life that I knew. Music is all that I've known since I was little.

How have Reba's childhood experiences affected her life style now?

Celebrity Witness

> I appreciate things more than a lot of the kids that are mad because they are not instant successes in contemporary music, Christian music, or whatever. When you grow up and you've slept in church basements or other people's homes, and lived on MacDonald's hamburgers that you split amongst yourselves, you appreciate airplanes that get you places. You still complain because that is human nature; but I do, I think, appreciate things a little more than some.

Reba describes her religious upbringing.

> My whole perspective on serving God was out of fear. If I didn't serve Him, He was going to zap me with some bad disease, or my mother was going to get sick or whatever. I was going to be on the slippery side of hell or something. Really. I went through the motions of serving Him, but it was almost 100 percent out of fear. It wasn't until I began to travel, meet other people, learn and go to other churches, that I began to realize the depth of His love and began to serve Him out of love and not out of fear. That is a totally different thing.

This life style did not nurture a healthy self-love in Reba. She comments:

> I grew up with a very poor opinion of myself. I was fat. I was real moody. I was a loner when I was growing up. My parents traveled and sang and I stayed with other people and always felt in the way. The Lord has helped me with my poor self-image. I thought I was very ugly. I thought I had a weird voice that nobody would ever like. The devil puts a lot of those things on you. The Lord has helped me to see that if I have a bad opinion of what He has made I don't have a good opinion of Him.

Reba Rambo

How have Reba's standards changed over the years?

Each one of us has standards because of our environment, church background and teaching. We have the standards of what "spiritual" is. One thing that has helped me sympathize with some people who have literally crucified me is that I can remember my background. I was raised in a very strict church. Everything was sin—no ballgames, girls were not allowed to wear pants, we couldn't cut our hair, we couldn't wear make-up, etc. Everything was sin. There were some people in our church who wouldn't drink Coca-Cola because they felt it was a sin. They wouldn't drink iced tea. It was that strict.

I can remember when I was ten, I traveled one weekend with a gospel group who were good friends of my family. Well, we had a day off and we stopped in a little town that had a little swimming pool. There were no other guests in the motel except this gospel-singing family. They decided to go swimming. The mother of the group came out and she had on a sleeveless sun dress, low-stranded pearls and some pink lipstick. I can remember excusing myself and going into my motel room and getting on my knees and just crying and crying and begging God to forgive those people for sinning so terribly bad.

At that stage in my life I didn't think you could be spiritual unless you had this ashen face and had long, long hair and long sleeves. It was almost like they had to be nun-like in appearance, before they could be spiritual. Now, from traveling and getting out in the world and reading the Word more, I don't feel that way. Everyone has his own standards of what "spiritual" is, but there are some people who try to gauge you according to their standards. That can be rough!

Celebrity Witness

Reba tells how her convictions have come to be her own, not second-hand convictions that belong to someone else.

> A lot of us really had honest convictions about our ministries, how we should handle things. We tried to put those same convictions on everyone else's ministries. And it didn't always work. There are people the Lord uses to reach other people that I could never reach. I have to open my own mail from God for my own ministry. They can't open it for me and read it for me. They'd read something different into it than I would. It has been hard for all of us to learn that, but everybody's ministry is not the same. We are learning, but a lot of us have really hard lessons to learn and some of us are still being really rough on the others. I stand back and I think, "Oh, Lord! I feel for them. The lessons you are going to have to teach them." He has to teach all of us these lessons. We have to learn these kinds of things: to be forgiving to one another, to understand and love in spite of whether or not we agree. There are other people, especially in contemporary Christian music, whom I don't agree with, especially in the way they handle their ministry. By the time I start to criticize I find myself saying, "Lord, maybe that is what you want them to do." So we are all having to learn to talk to the Lord about it if we don't agree, not to talk about other people. We need to lift them up and talk about things that are of good report, not about the bad.

Reba's music ministry is continually expanding. Who does she reach?

> I'd say I reach more junior and senior high school and college kids. It just seems to me that they can relate to my music. However, I may get a letter from a

seventy-year-old grandmother who says she likes my music. Young people can relate more to what I have to say because I can understand more what they are going through. I can't always sympathize with a fifty-year-old lady because I haven't gone through the things she has gone through. Most of the problems the young people have faced, I've faced, or something similar. The Word comes to life, whenever you feel like someone who is sharing His Word is there and you get a hold and see things in it that you never saw before. When you are sitting there and everything is going great, you say, "Oh, isn't that nice." When you are drowning, it is like reaching for a life preserver. It really is.

Besides ministering to Christians, Reba has been able to reach out to non-Christians as well.

I do some secular concerts. Most of the work I have done has been with B.J. Thomas. He is a Christian, but a lot of the concerts he does are not billed as Christian concerts. The first one we worked on I'll never forget. I was petrified. Nobody told me until we got there that it was not a Christian concert, as such. I knocked on his dressing room door and introduced myself. I said, "How long do you want me to sing?" He said, "Well, sing until you're done." And I replied, "Well, what do you want me to say?" He answered, "Just say what you always say." He just put me at ease.

When we work together, we usually do three songs back-to-back without talking. I just pick positive-message tunes that aren't real preachy. For example, tunes that stress Jesus saved my soul, the four spiritual laws, that kind of thing. I just sing real positive-message tunes and usually by the end of the third song, I figure they either like us or they

Celebrity Witness

don't. The music has either won them or it hasn't. Usually we'll say something like, "If you haven't figured out by now, we are a gospel group."

The kids will usually say, "Yeah, if that's what you are, that is fine." I've found that if you are honest in what you do, people will buy it. They can detect whether you are sincere in what you are doing or not. If you are devout, if you are really a Christian, most people will say, "Okay." The kids realize that we love what we are doing and we are sincere about it. Most of them are not offended; they are very curious and want to know more. As a matter of fact, I think we have had more conversions in secular concerts than Christian concerts because I usually say, "Hey, if you want to know more about what we are talking about, come backstage or pick out a band member and talk to him." Kids are searching for truth. They detect something different and they are very curious; and it has been a great opportunity to witness to people.

Judy Gossett, Reba's booking agent, tells how life has changed for them since Reba has gone out on her own.

When Reba decided she was going to go on her own, she thought the Lord was moving her apart from her family, from the professional standpoint only, not family-wise. Musically, we sat down and made a list. We made a list of things we wanted to achieve for the Lord. Things we decided we weren't going to do and things we were going to do. We decided when we had a band that every day we'd have compulsory Bible study and prayer time. Every musician we've ever hired has known that. Obviously, we didn't hire him if he wasn't willing to comply with that.

Reba Rambo

> Every day we've had Bible study and prayer with our band, not just before a concert, but a real fellowship with the Lord and with each other and even Scripture memorization. The Word becomes real life to people. It has been such a sustaining factor in Reba's ministry. For the most part, I don't remember one musician yet who hasn't thanked us for helping him grow in the Lord. That has been part of our contribution to the ministry.

Being in the public eye for so long, Reba is well-acquainted with the problems presented by the entertainment life style. She comments:

> The worst thing is a lot of people tend to put you on pedestals. You kind of wonder, "Did they really like me or did they like me for who they think I am or what they think I am?" It is not that you are putting yourself up there, but people do that to you. That is sad because people don't think you are human, that you have human problems and failures. It is difficult to establish any kind of a long-term relationship. I've had a career since I was thirteen; a lot of men feel threatened by that, having a woman that travels. I had a marriage that didn't succeed from a lot of different problems. One thing was just being on the road traveling. It is rough. It is hard on a man to cope with that kind of situation.

Not all people put entertainers on a pedestal. Many make a point of criticizing every move a celebrity makes. Reba explains:

> So many people I've been around make it a point to keep me humble. About the time you'd get proud, some person will walk up and say, "How dare you dress like that? How dare you do this or that?" They will devastate you. You couldn't be proud. You are

Celebrity Witness

just wondering, "What am I doing here?" I had a lady come up to me in the crowded lobby during intermission at one of my concerts. She walked up and said very loudly and in very poor taste, "Do you call that singing? You sound like somebody calling hogs." There was a lobby full of people, and you think that won't humble you! So about the time you get real proud and think you are sounding great, somebody will do something like that. It will just totally burst your balloon.

Reba shares about her divorce.

If there are two people hurting, it really doesn't matter whose fault it is. I've never seen a divorce when both persons were not somewhat involved. The fault really doesn't matter. The thing is still hurting. In the story about the rich man who was beaten and robbed, it really wasn't his fault. He was at the wrong place at the wrong time. But the bottom line was he was in the ditch dying and people walked by and said, "Look at him; he is a bad person." The problem was if Jesus hadn't come along, he would have lain there and died, whether or not it was his fault. As Christians we have to look past why people are hurting and just see the hurt and minister to that hurt. Who cares why they are hurting? They are dying. People need to just reach out with real compassion and forgiveness and understanding, and that is hard to do a lot of times.

Judy Gossett sheds some light on Reba's experience.

I think Reba, having gone through what she has in the past few years, has deepened her ministry. You never know what somebody is going through unless you go through it yourself. Then your ministry is broadened and deepened to include those people.

Reba Rambo

Reba continues:

When this first happened to me, I thought, "Lord, how are you ever going to get any glory out of this?" God didn't cause my divorce. But this has shown me more than anything else in life that, no matter what problem you face, God can turn it around and make some good out of it. In spite of the mistakes we make in our lives, He is so loving and kind and so magnificent. Whatever mess we get ourselves into, He can turn it around for good. I have been able to counsel or just cry with someone who is hurting from divorce. I don't have all the answers, but I can say I know that hurt.

I've had people literally walk up to me and say, "Reba, you are going to hell because of what you did." How do you cope with that? I say, "Hey, I've thrown myself on the mercy of God. In His eyes, divorce and murder are no different. They are both sin. He doesn't have a scale of one to ten." People can be so cruel. They think because you are on stage and you are a gospel singer or speaker or minister, etc., that you are above the problems of the world—but you are not.

They think certain sins or certain problems you have are unpardonable. A lot of times you have no control over situations. Sometimes they just happen and you say, "Lord, what is going on?" Oftentimes all you can do is cast yourself upon the Lord and say, "Lord, you be my strength and you be my forgiveness," and go on. Because if you do what the devil wants you to do, you'd throw up your hands. He made me want to crawl into a cave and die. I literally felt like that. You can't do that. That wouldn't be God's will.

Celebrity Witness

What would Reba's most prominent prayer request be?

> To have the wisdom of God from God. We have such a desire to literally reach the world. I pray and I believe that the doors are opening more for us to reach the lost and not the found.

Reba explains her feelings further.

> We've carried water forever to the sea instead of the desert. Like contemporary Christian music, a lot of us have had visions of being on secular radio and all, but we weren't ready for that. We weren't good enough. The records weren't good enough to compete for number one. I think now they are. I think now the Lord is grooming us to represent Him more and more to the unsaved. Also, many in secular music have become Christians. He is going to have people in there witnessing to those kids. He is going to do it.

What does Reba see for the future?

> My main dream is to reach the world. I love my Christian brothers and sisters and I need them to support me and to help me. I don't know exactly how He is going to do all this, but I'm excited about what He is going to do.

Reba is in the process of reaching the world for Christ. Her travels have already brought her overseas.

> We've done several television specials overseas. They invited us over to sing. They really didn't realize what they were getting into as we'd sing. In these cathedral-type churches, with stained glass, the people could come in. They knew us from the TV shows. As we began to sing we'd raise our hands. This is just us. We were trying to behave ourselves.

Reba Rambo

Just every now and then, the people would kind of look around and barely sneak a little hand up. Then we'd give an invitation. Those people would sit with their mouths open because they had never seen anything like it. So many people were won to the Lord. The people that brought us over began to realize what was going on and they got highly upset about our being there and doing that sort of thing. That door has kind of been closed since then. The Lord is going to open that door again because the Dutch people are really hungry for the Lord. I really want to sing and minister to people like that because it is new to them; it isn't old hat.

Cheryl and Terry Blackwood

14
Cheryl and Terry Blackwood

Cheryl and Terry Blackwood are probably best known for their individual contributions to the music industry. Cheryl, in her role as Miss America 1980, has come to the forefront as a Christian spokeswoman as well as an accomplished musician. Her first album, "I'm a Miracle," combines the gospel message with her vocal abilities. *A Bright Shining Place,* Cheryl's autobiography, traces her life as a youngster with a dream in her heart to become Miss America. A crippling accident almost shattered her dream, but God's overcoming power proved to be victorious in Cheryl's life.

Terry is the son of the late Doyle Blackwood, one of the original Blackwood Brothers. With a background steeped in gospel music, Terry first made his mark in the award-winning gospel group, "The Imperials." Terry later branched off with a member of the group, Sherman Andrus, to form the contemporary gospel group, Andrus, Blackwood and Company.

With their marriage on April 19, 1981, Cheryl and Terry embarked on a life together that has already combined their unique talents and abilities. A seven-year courtship provided much stability for the pressures inherent in any celebrity marriage. Cheryl and Terry offer advice to those who are determined to succeed in marriage in the following conversation.

Celebrity Witness

Cheryl: I think that first and foremost, the thing that should be said and done in every Christian marriage for the couple to stay together is to put their marriage above everything else in their lives. Their ministries, their careers, even their families and their friends. Nothing should go above their marriage. Their ministries should not go above their marriage because God wouldn't have marriages destroyed. It's just like the Word says, when God was talking to a man who wanted to be a leader of a church. God said, "You cannot handle your own children; how can you handle my children?" So I think it's the same thing in a marriage. If we want to teach other people how to do this and how to do that, we must live like the Lord tells us to live. If we can't even be that wife or that husband that God has told us to be, we have no right or place to teach anybody else how to do anything. So, without a happy marriage, we don't have a ministry. We may try to fool ourselves into thinking we do, but we don't.

Terry: The really meaningful, important things in life require a certain amount of diligence and discipline and effort and that's what our commitment is all about. Our own individual relationship with Jesus is first in our lives, then our commitment to one another—our marriage vows—that is to love, honor and cherish, until death do us part. We believe that this is forever. It's not until times get a little tough.

Cheryl: You continually think there is no other way. There is not an option to this, so you make it work. A point that is very vital from the woman's standpoint is that Christ is first, the husband is under Christ and the wife is under the husband. People in today's age don't want to think that way, but that's the way God set it up and that's the way it has to be to work. A lot of wives will say, "Well, if my husband was doing what the Word says and treating me like Christ treats the church, then it would be easy for me to treat him like Christ." But the fact is, we can't worry about how the other person works. Christ tells me, as a wife, to treat Terry as I treat Christ. In other words, to adore him, to reverence him, to love him, just like I love Christ, because he's my head. In return, Terry is supposed to, and does, love me as Christ loves the church—with protection, and every move is for my good. [He] sets up everything in my behalf just like Christ did. I'm supposed to be what God called me to be. I do not answer for Terry being what he's supposed to be as a husband. I answer for being the wife that I'm supposed to be and then God takes care of the rest.

Terry: Then God takes care of me if I'm not doing my job, because He's my authority.

Cheryl: I think the Christian world is starving for some good marriage role models. They want it so badly. The longer we're married, the more it speaks to people that we're going to stay married. We speak out about our happiness and about what we have to work through. It's not a fairy tale and you have to work at it. They seem to want to hear that—and we do seem to get more engagements because of it.

Terry: Of course, the role model is certainly a heavy responsibility, and I don't even know if we realize that responsibility fully. We approach this very humbly, knowing we're only human. Satan is even probably more bent on putting problems in our marriage. That's why when people come up and they ask me about our marriage, they're really pleased and thrilled to see it working. We just tell them it's just the grace of God and I almost invariably will ask them to pray for us. Because, without the prayers of those people, we could be involved in serious problems just like many other marriages seem to be in.

Cheryl: Of course, Satan's tried temptations, but they kind of bounced off us because they really weren't temptations. We waited so long to have each other that no other man or no

Celebrity Witness

other woman has even been a temptation in our marriage. So, from that standpoint, I don't think he even bothers with us because he knows he's wasting his time.

Terry: At that one point, we are so sure. It's not like you go into a marriage, . . . wondering if this is the one. But, after seven years, and after all the things that have happened, we had no doubt in our minds.

Cheryl: We have a twenty- or thirty-year marriage trust. We trust each other so much because we were together for so long before we married. We went through so many of the things that people go through after they were married. We were so much more sure of each other. I was not just sure of my love for Terry, I knew he was 100 percent committed to me when we got married. So those things, Satan cannot even tempt us with.

The things he's [Satan] tried to work on in us involve our family. He would just cause us to have our thoughts to be on something else rather than on building our marriage. Our thoughts would be on record contracts or book contracts or health problems in the family. Just nitpicky things—the cares of life. Little things that normally would not bother you, but enough of them begin to take away from the time that you'd spend with each other. It may come to a point where we need to take real authority over these things.

For a year, when we went to bed was the first time we'd talk all day long. That is one of the hardest things in a marriage—communication. When you get to the bottom line, when you communicate, you virtually have 100 percent less problems than you have when you don't communicate, so we did communicate. But, we invariably did it at four in the morning instead of at a normal time. We always need to recognize the source of our problems. Satan is the source of them. Go directly to the source of the problem and be mad at that instead of being mad at whoever he used to be the problem.

Cheryl and Terry Blackwood

The Blackwoods' marriage relationship stands out in the face of rising divorce statistics among entertainers in the Christian community. They both are greatly disturbed about this new trend.

Cheryl: I want to say, "Work things out." I don't even care if they were right for each other in the beginning. I think we have a ministry to Christian marriages that are falling apart. Inevitably, the Lord seems to put us in their lives to try to give them the strength to stay together, to keep working at it. It's usually not the couple, it's usually one partner or the other. We wind up saying, "One of you has got to stay with it, one of you has got to work. Both of you need to, but one has to."

Terry: With couples who are in the public eye, there is an unusual amount of ego involved. There's a lot of selfishness, and problems in marriage where one wants his way, maybe even at the expense of the other. There's not the feeling, "Well, if I get my way, will that hurt my wife?" or "How will she respond to that?" rather than, "What can I do to make sure that our commitment and our relationship is solid? If I do this, will that affect that relationship?" I think they're just too anxious to do their own thing even at the expense of the other person, and frankly no job is worth breaking up a marriage over. No job.

Cheryl: We've been offered several things that we've had to very carefully contemplate how those things would affect our partner. If we didn't do that, we could have been destroyed ten times by now. When we went into it, it was with the idea that our marriage, our commitment to one another, would take priority over our ministries and our touring schedules. We always consult one another when we get a booking to see if it's okay with the other one. We're able to set our schedules according to what's best for our marriage.

Celebrity Witness

Terry: I'll admit that Cheryl is a giver much more than I am. When you're thirty-seven and you've never married, you're pretty self-centered and that's something I work on a lot. She is so giving that she would probably never take anything if she knew that it would be something that I would have a problem with. She has always consulted me with a decision. That has tended to make me want to say, "Well, honey, I want you to do what you want to do." Of course, as long as it doesn't hurt her and us, or keep us apart. I think that's the main thing. If it takes one person from the other one, for any length of time, it can't be good. It's critical, it's vital to be together. You don't have to be together every day, but keep that open line of communication.

Cheryl and Terry have suffered little of the criticism that many of the entertainers in the Christian community have had to deal with.

Cheryl: The only criticism that I can think of, in the entire time I've been traveling and ministering, was from a man who told me I needed to curb my taste in clothes. And he was right. Terry had been working on me for three or four months at the time and I hadn't known. You know, you come out of the pageant scene and you've got all these pageant clothes that you don't know what to do with them. Now, I'm going to sell most of them. But he was speaking from the point of view of men who were looking to me as a minister. On every hand I was the person they needed to see unless I wore the wrong thing. They couldn't even hear what I had to say because they were looking at the dress that I wore, an outfit that was not necessarily godly.

The Word tells us it's our responsibility. If we are offended, to at least discuss that offensiveness with that person and allow them to know that they are doing something that is causing some type of confusion.

Cheryl and Terry Blackwood

Terry: Not 100 percent of the people have ulterior, selfish motives when they're critical. Sometimes they really are genuinely concerned and maybe God has placed you on their heart for a specific reason.

Cheryl: I think any type of Christian celebrity is in a position of "to whom much is given, much is required." Underline the word "much." *Much* is required. Because our lives are affecting many, many other lives, we have to be even more aware and even more concerned and even more cautious than anybody else. If we don't meet that requirement, all will be taken away, I believe. Even though we may not see it at first, I believe that the time will come.

Terry: I have heard it said to avoid the very appearance of evil. Even if they are not evil, if they appear to be evil, we're to avoid them.

Cheryl: Just like the company we keep is also extremely important. Why be so headstrong and bent on wearing clothes that might be offensive to somebody else, when I can just get something that isn't offensive to somebody else? It all just comes down to one thing: if people would truly live their lives by the Word, there wouldn't be all this controversy. Because there's only one way to live your life and that's like Christ lived His. If we're not bringing people to Jesus, we're doing the wrong thing. People can get so screwed up when they have a form of religion, but don't have the true Christ living in their heart, to tell them what's true and what isn't. When you know the Word, about one-half of the time, you already know the answer.

Terry: The whole thing involves growing into the perfect man that God has in mind for all of us to be. To be the overcomer that we all are supposed to be. That's what it's all about.

Celebrity Witness

Overall, fame hasn't affected the Blackwood's life style in many concrete ways, other than financially.

Cheryl: I buy more expensive clothes, I drive a better car. I used to drive a Plymouth and now I drive a BMW. Used to wear a rabbit and now I wear a mink. I still talk the same, I still feel the same, I'm still tight as a bark on a tree.

Terry: I think coming from a poor family, as we both did, we're not really what you'd call extravagant.

Cheryl: For example, we fuss about the light bill. We keep the heat down low.

Terry: We still appreciate the nice things. We can buy almost anything we want, but we don't buy it just because we have the money. We're expected to be good stewards of our money too. As far as fame, I've had to talk myself into having any degree of self-confidence at all, which is why she's in my life, I'm sure, to help me with my self-image. I came from a place in my own life where I couldn't believe anybody would take the time to want my autograph. But I'm 100 percent better than I was two years ago. Now, that particular thing destroys a lot of people. You know, they begin to believe all the public relations. I really thank the Lord because I can't personally see where it [fame] has affected me at all. In fact, if anything, it's helped me be more well-rounded, more balanced because I felt so inferior for so long. About Cheryl, I know her well enough to know that she could go back to teaching tomorrow and would love it because if the doors closed to her ministry, she'd know that it was what God had for her. It's no big deal. It's easy come, easy go.

Cheryl: I don't feel any different now than I felt when I was teaching school. I have not changed any of the part of me that's really me. I've grown up and I'm older and I think maybe

Cheryl and Terry Blackwood

a little differently. But I feel the same way, I'm just dealing with a little more cash, but I do it the same way I did before. I just have more to give now and as long as I've got it, I'm going to give it too.

Terry: I think God has found that He can trust us with more than He used to trust us with, and I think we're both at the point in our lives, if we feel God wants us to give a certain amount of money to someone else, we just give it. I feel like now, it's a thrill to give more.

Cheryl: Many times the Lord will speak to us both. We both have felt a real need to support those who can't support themselves, which is usually older people. We support six couples a month. We've asked them to pray one hour a day for our ministry and when people do get saved and healed and Spirit-filled in our ministry, it's as much to their credit as to ours for being the prayer warriors.

Terry shares his prayer request for their marriage.

Terry: For one thing, we would desire the mind of Christ—wisdom and understanding to know what the voice of God is—when He's speaking, when to move—to have the mind of Christ in every decision we make.

Andrae Crouch

15
Andrae Crouch

Andrae Crouch was the leader of the group, "Andrae Crouch and the Disciples," that pioneered in contemporary Christian music. Crouch and his band have been nominated for eleven Grammy Awards and they have received three. Crouch's music was considered controversial. He took basic rock 'n roll, rhythm-and-blues arrangements and combined them with gospel lyrics. Criticized in conventional Christian circles, Crouch's music has ministered to individuals around the globe. Together since 1966, the group's bookings have taken them from small churches to the world's leading concert halls. The group has also received secular recognition. Television appearances on such shows as *The Tonight Show, Dinah, Mike Douglas* and *Saturday Night Live* were not uncommon.

Crouch has won more recognition from secular musicians than has any other gospel artist and his compositions have been recorded by such stars as Diana Ross, Elvis Presley, Paul Simon and Barbara Mandrell. Crouch has been a "crossover" artist when his gospel music made the popular music charts.

Crouch broke away from his back-up group about four years ago to go out on his own and get some rest. He hasn't rejected the contemporary Christian music field, though.

Celebrity Witness

It's growing so fast because Christians aren't a minority any more. Nowadays, people everywhere are born again. There are millions of us now. You have Christian radio stations, stores, music, movies—you have Christian everything.

How has fame affected Crouch's life?

First of all, I appreciate all the people in the families I've met. It is really rough on a person when he's popular because some people see him only as a song, not as a person. People know I'm in the ministry, but I think as a person. A singer or minister is limited by the fact that people only want to respond to a person for what he does and not for who he is. That gets to be weird sometimes.

Do Crouch's fans see him as a person at all?

I love to go boating and I love fishing. I love animals and I have a collection of mammals and things like that; but the average person doesn't know that. To them, I'm just a song. I'm my last album. I'm also spiritual, however. Many times I write a song because I think it is a good idea. I think people will enjoy it in their homes. I think it will bring a certain amount of teaching to them. Not all the time is it where I am. I might be writing it for them, thinking maybe that is where they are. So it's kind of frustrating in this way.

Does Crouch make musical decisions according to the comments of other Christians, or does the Lord inspire him in everything?

I think my musical decisions have been affected both ways. Certainly, I listen to everything. Now I'm studying at a mission youth leadership training center in Hawaii. I'm raising money for that. I've had

Andrae Crouch

a lot of good Bible teaching and support from people. I think it is most important. I get it from people. I really value their comments and their leadership in regard to some things I do, which sometimes might be negative and sometimes might be positive. I listen to what they say, so I've had good teaching. I think the church has run away a lot of good talent because the other people might not have been as strong as I and they were just lovers of the Lord and they love music and they didn't want to be stifled. Because of that, their kind of music was just thrown out. It is unfortunate and I feel for these people. I want to support some of them and help them see what they should do and that kind of thing.

Part III

Talk Show Personalities

Art Linkletter

16
Art Linkletter

Art Linkletter is a household name in America. The host of two of the longest running shows in broadcasting history, *People Are Funny* and *House Party,* Linkletter is also the respected author of several books. He is one of the foremost crusaders against drug abuse in the United States. This personal crusade against drug abuse has earned Linkletter a seat on the President's National Advisory Council for Drug Abuse Prevention and on the National Coordinating Council on Drug Abuse Education and Information, Inc.

Linkletter has been awarded seven honorary doctoral degrees from colleges and universities for his humanitarian work and interest in youth.

Arthur Gordon Linkletter was born in Saskatchewan, Canada. An orphan, he was adopted by a Baptist evangelist and his wife. An English major in college, Linkletter intended to become a college professor. During his senior year in college, Linkletter was offered a job as a radio announcer, and as a result of this he decided to remain in the broadcasting industry after graduation.

Linkletter has now been in broadcasting for over forty years. His show, *People Are Funny,* was on NBC-TV and radio for nineteen years. *House Party* ran on CBS-TV and radio for twenty-five years, and was one of the top daytime shows from its beginning. The show won one Emmy Award and was

Celebrity Witness

nominated for several others. Linkletter has since starred in and co-produced many spectaculars and specials, as well as having appeared in a half-dozen dramatic shows and several motion pictures.

When did Linkletter first become aware of the presence of God?

> I don't know because I was adopted by a minister and I can never remember when we didn't pray and read the Bible. In fact, my father lived a twenty-four-hour working day of Christian belief. He was the most devout man I've ever met. From my earliest days I really thought that my father had written the Bible because he had it memorized.

Linkletter explains how he first became involved with show business:

> I was going to college studying to be an English teacher. It was during the Depression and I was taking all kinds of jobs. I had written a musical comedy for the college, and the local radio station manager had seen it and heard it. He called the professor of the college who was in charge of the faculty broadcasting on that station. I was very active—a debater, a public speaker, president of the student body and all that; so he recommended me. I was making Waldorf salads in the cafeteria at lunch, working my way through day and night. The call came through, did I want to be a radio announcer? And I said, "Certainly." I had never thought of it, but I always said yes to everything. So then I was given the job as a radio announcer; and by the time I finished college, a year and a half later, I was making more money than I would have made as a teacher. I was making $125 a month. The school teaching job paid $120 a month.

Art Linkletter

Of all of Linkletter's achievements, which ones mean the most to him?

> Looking back over my life, the most thrilling thing would be my first big national show, *People Are Funny.* Actually, it has to be your first thrill. This is when you reach the top. Then the next thrill would be winning the Emmy Award for the best television show. Then when I won the Grammy Award for the best record, and appearances like the one at the United Nations on drug abuse, or the first time I appeared with President Eisenhower at a White House dinner before everybody who matters—those kind of things.

Linkletter talks about the kind of standards he has followed during his years in show business.

> To begin with, I will not play any part or participate in any program which is demeaning or immoral or cheap or represents me as anything other than a reasonably nice, constructive person. I just don't feel comfortable and I wouldn't even think of it. I've been offered parts like that. Even parts in which I would be portrayed as ridiculous—like a Jerry Lewis part—a zany part, a crazy part. I don't feel comfortable. I am not an actor. I'm a communicator. Also, I wouldn't be in any type of stunt show that is demeaning to other people.

He describes how the broadcasting industry has changed over the years.

> At the start, all broadcasting was very straight. When I started in broadcasting, you couldn't even use the word *dam* to describe a river that had been blocked. You couldn't use the word *pregnant.* You would be cut right off the air. I spent a good many

Celebrity Witness

years of my life in broadcasting when it was taboo to say or do anything that was the least bit immoral. Of course my own background and upbringing made me shy away from the double entendre and so-called smart-alec smutty stuff. Early on, when I said something that was funny but had a little edge to it, I would get some letters from people who said they were disappointed in me. They had felt that I would never stoop to that kind of thing. I realized right then and there that there were so many good things to talk about and so much fun on a high level, why risk offending anybody? It isn't as if you were stuck with that kind of material. I also realized, after doing some personal appearances in the strictly show business dinners, where everybody is being a little bit over the line, that people will laugh at you and applaud you in a meeting and then on the way home, they will criticize you.

Linkletter explains why he no longer attends the Hollywood dinner parties.

You see, they'll go along with the crowd, but there will be a certain number of people who don't like it. I don't like it either. As a matter of fact, in the last ten to twelve years, I haven't even been to those kinds of dinners. The last time I went was to a dinner for Milton Berle. Pearl Bailey and I sat next to each other. Pearl is a good Christian, and she and I decided that we'd either get up and leave that night or we'd never come back again to be subjected to that kind of language, much less saying it.

Even though Linkletter has not attended these parties, he still finds acceptance among his colleagues.

I find no difference in people's regard of me any more than they do about my not drinking. A lot of

Art Linkletter

> people say you have to drink if you are at a party, especially those with sophisticated Hollywood stars. If you are not drinking, they say you are a party pooper. I find none of that. They know I don't drink. The bartenders automatically pour me some ginger ale and there is nothing said. I don't make excuses. I don't say anything except that I don't drink.

Enduring relationships are relatively rare in the entertainment community. Linkletter is one of the few Hollywood stars who has had a stable marriage. He talks about his happy marriage of forty-six years.

> She was in high school and I was in college. She was never in show business. She is a very private person. My wife is not an outgoing person; she is the guardian of the castle; she is the mother, the handiworker. She does nameless things with jewelry and with painting, those kinds of things.

Linkletter tells of how his wife brings a balance to his life.

> She gives me the other side. After the shock of public adulation, she keeps me on a level keel. You'll get a kick out of this. One night we were coming home and I had just received a giant award by Christians and Jews. On the way home I said to her, "There are not too many people in the world that deserve this kind of award." She said, "I think there is one less than you do." She keeps my head in the proper perspective.

Linkletter had four children that were the pride of his life. Since 1969, two of them have had tragic deaths. How did Linkletter endure these tragedies?

> I would have to say, first, it is the belief that they are somewhere and that I will join them. That is the greatest source, knowing they are with the Lord. If

you just thought they were gone like moths or flies that died, it would all seem so useless. Secondly, you have to have some kind of faith that there is a plan bigger than you can see, because you can't possibly see any reason for something like this happening. You've got to believe there is one or else it is unsupportable.

Linkletter acknowledges that his belief in God has sustained him through the tragedies of his life. What is his biggest frustration today?

The most painful frustration is working in the drug-abuse scene and seeing people lost that I thought were saved. I spend time with families and people, I work with them and suddenly they are back. This tends to burn me up. It is called "burn out" in social work.

What type of prayer request would Linkletter ask from other Christians?

I would ask to be sustained in my struggle against the overwhelming amount of negatives. For instance, after twelve years of many fine people working in drug-abuse control, there is more drug abuse than ever. If you just take those figures, you'd say, "What's the use? I quit!" You have to keep trying. The prayers to sustain me in my effort is what I need.

In what ways does Linkletter think fame has affected his life?

For me, it has made me more aware of my responsibility as an example. It is like a responsible parent who is made better by his children's eyes on him because he knows they will not do as he says, but as he does. So, with the eyes of the nation on me, I am inclined to make a better choice of two decisions, knowing it is my responsibility. We are all human and we are all subject to temptations of all kinds. Sometimes when I have been tempted to go one way or the other, I would say, "If this were Mickey Rooney doing it and if he were publicized doing it, nobody would care, but they would care if it was me."

With a wealth of experience behind him, what does Linkletter hope for the future?

I hope just to do what I'm doing better. You can always make better choices, do things better. If you didn't think you were going to do anything better, it would be pretty bleak. If a world champion pole vaulter quits, he is washed up. He has got to say, "I've broken the record; now what more can I do?" I'm much the same way.

Linkletter is currently active in several projects but does not want to be tied down to a regular series in the future.

I have been asked to do a number of shows and I would conceivably do an insert on a magazine show where they want me to do some kid things. If I could do about ten to twelve segments in one afternoon and if they can dribble it out over a month, then I would participate in the show; but I would not go into a regular series.

Treena and Graham Kerr

17
Graham and Treena Kerr

For many years, Graham and Treena Kerr have been known as personalities in the secular television industry. Their program, *The Galloping Gourmet,* was shown all over the world. Six years ago, the Kerrs were worth millions of dollars. When they became Christians, the distributors of their program refused to let them integrate their new faith into the show. The Kerrs resigned from their contract, resulting in a personal relinquishment of over $3 million.

During the first two years they were Christians, the Kerrs appeared on over 200 talk shows with an audience of over 400 million people. Because of the immediate and widespread exploitation, the Kerrs soon became turned off to television. Since that time, they have done very few Christian media appearances; they did not even own a television set until 1983.

Since 1982 Treena has become an international Bible teacher, ministering "healing of attitudes" to women's groups. Graham works in the area of "creative life styles," teaching how to "live better for less" and to share the surplus with those in need.

Treena explains how she came to know the Lord.

> I was about to be committed to a mental institution. I didn't know it, but Graham had been given the word. I was very violent. I was on drugs. I had

Celebrity Witness

reached forty. We had everything of materialistic need in the world, except a good relationship with our children and with each other.

I had a black maid working for us. Unbeknown to me, she and her whole black church in Wilmington, Delaware, prayed for me for three months. I didn't believe in Jesus. I was on yoga, meditation, and cards and anything you can think of to try to get peace. I'd been searching to be loved for me, without having to perform all my life, but it never seemed that could be.

One day I told Ruthie [the maid] that I couldn't take things anymore. I didn't love anybody and everybody was scared stiff of me because I had a very, very violent temper. I also had a very filthy mouth. I swore a lot and cussed a lot. Ruthie said to me, "Well, Mrs. Kerr, why don't you take your problems to God?" So I said, "Okay, God, you take them because I can't do it anymore." That was on a Tuesday. On Friday that week, Ruthie said, "Have you thought of getting baptized?" I said, "No." She suggested that I be baptized and I said that I didn't believe in Jesus. As I said that, a little voice in my head said, "But when you lose your temper, you always go and wash yourself or go for a swim, so why not try the water?" I pulled back and said, "Okay, I'll get baptized on Tuesday."

Graham was away. If anyone knew I was going to do this, they'd know I was crazy, so we didn't tell anybody. I went to a little black church, outside eastern Maryland, at a place called Bethlehem, and the pastor's name was Friend. He asked me if I knew what I was doing and I said I wouldn't be there if I didn't, which was a lie. He said, "Well, you may not receive it today." And I said, "Yes, I will." Ruthie said, "Yes, she is ready for it." So they all prayed and thanked God for the new soul and thanked Him that

Graham and Treena Kerr

all the angels in heaven were going to rejoice.

I had a very extraordinary experience. Before I got to the water, I was literally pushed onto my knees. As my knees touched the ground, I had this water pouring out of my eyes. It wasn't tears. It was just pouring out and I was saying, "Thank you, Jesus. Forgive me Jesus. I'm sorry Jesus." I had only used Jesus' name as a curse word before this. Every time I was saying this out loud, I got this terrible pain inside my heart. Suddenly the water stopped and I got up.

Nobody noticed what had happened to me. They put me in the water when they stopped praying. They asked me if I'd like to tarry, so I said, "I might as well, as long as I'm here." I knelt down because they said you kneel down and thank Jesus for the gift He is going to give you. I knelt down and thanked Jesus, who I did not believe in.

The sweat was literally pouring off my face. Suddenly, a bright light came upon my face and I opened my eyes, because I thought they'd turned the church lights up to make me think I was getting what I was supposed to be getting. There in front of me was an incredibly beautiful man, who smiled on me with the perfection of all relationships like a baby's smile, which is pure and real. I knew He loved me, and I hadn't done anything for it. He leaned forward and put His hand on my heart. I didn't know what had happened. The pastor said, "Have you received it?" I said I didn't know, but I'd seen someone.

What happened to Treena after this experience?

I'd been taking sleeping pills. I was a drug addict at the time. As I was about to take some sleeping pills that night, the Lord said, "You don't need those." So I threw every pill I had in the house down the lavatory, everything, all the speed I had, all the high pills, the

Celebrity Witness

low pills, everything. Then I started to read the Bible, which I'd bought on the previous Saturday because Ruthie had told me to. I knew that the man I'd seen at the church was Jesus. From that moment on, I was healed of my temper, my drug addiction and my violent nature. My whole life was completely turned around because I knew I was loved for Treena and not for anything that I had done or had to do.

What was Graham's reaction to the change in Treena?

I came home about three or four days after this took place. Treena had been told by the Lord not to say anything to me. She didn't. So I very interestingly wondered why everything was so peaceful. I wasn't given the reason for it. Two weeks later, a lady in the supermarket told me that she'd been baptized in the same way that Treena had. I came back and confronted Treena with this as a joke. She told me that it was true. I asked her whether she wanted me to be a Christian, because I was perfectly willing to give it a go. I'd tried everything else to get our relationship straight. It wouldn't have meant any kind of personal commitment from me at all. It would have been, "Yes, let's try something else." She said, "I need Jesus, but I don't know about you. Why don't you ask God about that yourself?" I didn't ask God about myself, but what I did do was start to watch Treena. She'd tried a lot of things before and they hadn't worked. So I was wondering how quickly this would fall apart.

It didn't fall apart. Two months later, the doctor came to see me, and when he told me that she would have to go away, he sat in my office and wept. He said, "She is a miracle." He was a Catholic. I went home and said, "All right, God. If this is your miracle, then I want what Treena has, too, because I would

Graham and Treena Kerr

> like that contentment which she has." Nothing happened. Months later, I just went down on my knees in real frustration and shouted out to God, "What do I have to say to you to get to know you like Treena does?" The only words I could come out with were, "Jesus, I love you." For me, I felt love back, straight away. Two and a half years later I stopped following Treena and started following Jesus.

Treena and Graham describe their marriage before becoming Christians. Graham admitted that they had come to the end.

> The one thing that was specifically, very interestingly, alive was the desire to remain together. The thought of divorce seemed to be personal; it seemed to be very selfish. The thought of being divorced hurt a great deal. Since I didn't know the Lord, I couldn't understand how much He hates divorce. I couldn't interpret my feelings as the fact that God hates it; I was just hating the idea. What I thought was, "I can't live without her." He is right. We have seen people divorced and remarried. They say, "Jesus is lovely. He gave me a terrific second marriage." And yet there are some deep wounds there. Those people are still bleeding badly. I was just so desperate to keep my marriage together.

Treena explains her view of the marriage.

> I walked out on Graham two or three times. God had given me a sense of humor. Graham would come after me always in the most extraordinary manner. I'd always find it very funny. I had a real heart for comedy and I could always see the funny side. I don't think I really thought of divorce. The only thing you are thinking is "getting your own back on the other one." I want to hurt. I always react, so

maybe when a person hurts someone else, the instinct is retaliation—even from the guy's point of view with the woman, if she has really hurt him.

Anyway, I never thought of divorce as divorce. I just wanted to get out. I was fed up with it, but when I started to think about it, I thought nobody else is going to put up with me anyway; so I might as well stay in the fire I'm used to.

After working out a damaged marriage, the Kerrs offer some advice they think would help someone today. Treena comments:

Ephesians 5. Some of the most important words in that are man nourishes and cherishes his wife as he does his own body. There is a lot of love mentioned in there. The word *cherish* means to keep deeply in mind, as Jesus does the church. And that means to be merciful, to be compassionate, to be gentle, to be loving, to listen and relisten, to take notice, to have her, rather than a whole group of men, number one in your life. Pray together. Keep her deeply in mind like Jesus does the church, and if you do that, you won't forget her name. You won't forget to mention her name to someone else. That is where hurts start in a marriage. "This is my lovely wife. My lovely wife does this and that." When a woman is just on one side like a shadow, the wife doesn't have a name. God made them one flesh. In the garden, before sin, they were equal. He made them equal.

It was sin that made man rule over her. Jesus came to stop that. There is an equality in the spirit; but men are physically stronger and men do have the final responsibility, not because they have the authority, but because they are the representatives of Jesus Christ. The more like Jesus the servant they become, the more respect and the more real submission they

Graham and Treena Kerr

have from their wives. It can't be helped; it happens naturally—I should say, supernaturally.

Graham adds to this:

It's funny how everybody does that. You introduce somebody as "my wife." I do that. Wives are wonderfully glossed over with that sweet smile, yet they are totally bleeding to death.

Treena continues:

We mentioned this to a guy on television once. The next day we were on his television program. He said "my wife, April." He looked at me in amazement. She was sitting off the set in the same corner she usually did because she was helping him. She had tears flowing down her long, drawn face. With three years on television she had never been mentioned by name, except as "my wife," "my lovely wife," "my dear wife," "my helping wife," etc. You know, God calls us by name, at least man can. The funny part about it was that man did name his wife; he called her Eve. Adam was allowed to name everything.

The Kerrs now have a renewed relationship. Graham comments:

We have a new title. It is called "guardian." I'm a guardian of Treena's faith and Treena is a guardian of mine. It is quite extraordinary. We go out together. I'll get hurt and Treena will not be. She'll get hurt and I'll still be able to see something. We can be ministers one to another.

Treena adds to this.

We tell each other the truth after praying. That is the important thing to do. Not to pray manipulative prayer, which we hear a lot of now. People haven't

Celebrity Witness

got the guts to say it outright, so they say it in a prayer in a very religious way. Prayer is one of the most important things Jesus has given us, and it is used as a manipulative thing to get back at someone.

Graham gives an example.

"A very gentle spirit. Give my husband a very gentle spirit." Right in front of him. Just sitting there and expecting God to work.

Treena offers a solution.

The best thing is to say, "God, I've really blown it and I ask your forgiveness now." Then, you will be cleansed. But one *must*, because of the pain we cause the Lord and others—and really repent.

How does it work in the Kerr's marriage?

When we see each other doing something or saying something or going off, God has given us the ability to be truthful with one another. This is a blessing. I think this is a gift because it could get out of hand. I think God just balanced us very, very quickly so we can be truthful with one another. We pray about it first and it all works out. God gave us each other. We know each other very well. In fact, sometimes I know Graham better inside than he does. He knows me better inside than I do. But God knows us both inside even better.

Part IV

A Different Type of Celebrity

The Reverend Jack Hayford

18
The Reverend Jack Hayford

The Reverend Jack Hayford is pastor of The Church On The Way in Van Nuys, California. When Hayford came to the church in 1969, there were only eighteen members. By the time the Pat Boone family joined the congregation, there were 150 members. Now each Sunday between 4,000 and 5,000 people attend services at the church.

Why does Hayford think so many celebrities attend his church?

> I think that the principal reason that there is any unusual number of celebrities in our congregation is because of the location. It is just over the hill from Beverly Hills and Bel-Air and Brentwood. Many people live in the San Fernando Valley where our church is. If you just touch a cross section of the community, there is a certain number of people in the entertainment industry you are going to touch. I think it is more reflective that we are touching our community. As far as why our church has them, I think if there is any single reason it is the emphasis on the Word of God. That is why other people come. People want to grow. We do not attract people who are looking for a show. A lot of the entertainers just want the opportunity to be a human being.

Celebrity Witness

Hayford talks about how the church is not intentionally celebrity oriented.

> The church grew up with renowned people involved in its life. As a result of that, there has been the ability of the people to pretty well acclimate themselves to the entertainers and renowned personalities as brothers and sisters in Christ. I think that as others come in who are new to the congregation and are well-known, it tends not to be so much a novelty and gives the people the opportunity just to be a part of the crowd.
>
> There is another factor that I don't know how to explain. I know there is something of the hand of God in that particular place. I don't presume to understand that at all, but I know it is a peculiar thing. While there are other churches in our community with well-known people because it is characteristic of the area, there is nonetheless an unusual selection of people in our church.

Celebrities do find personal ministry at the church. As a result of a special prayer meeting among the entertainers in February 1980, there has been a continued body ministry among the celebrities themselves.

> We never really made a distinct effort to set up a separate prayer group, nor was that anything I intended to continue functioning. The occasion came about when I had been feeling quite strongly that there was a real attack coming on these people in the spiritual realm. I called several of the well-known in our church together. We had a dinner in the conference room of my office. I set before them the very heavy charge. It was no small meeting, not a gentle exhortation; but as their pastor, I really nailed five main things down. These were things you can

The Reverend Jack Hayford

> present to anybody, but I felt this group of people needed to confront these things in a deep way.
>
> Since that time, there have been real broad attacks on most of them, in different ways. There has been really good resiliency; but they were really vicious attacks, things that were from within their families and from physical attacks. For example, one was nearly killed in an accident and God miraculously spared him. There have been a number of things that God has manifested His hand toward. I believe that preparedness for that, even last February, was crucial.

Although Hayford never intended for those meetings to continue functioning, they do on a limited basis. Efrem Zimbalist, for example, comments that the celebrities feel free to call each other day or night and have prayer meetings in times of need. Hayford responds:

> It really is important in a certain sense, that these people have the opportunity for developing some in-depth relationships with people who understand their circumstances, because it is really a unique set of circumstaces these people live in. It takes a certain largeness on the part of most people to be around them and not feel awed or impressed. Needless to say, the stars don't want anyone to feel that way but people tend to. Besides the fact they are all very nice people, they are remarkable, gifted people in every way. They are not "stars" by accident; they are people of unusual gifts.

Hayford, being a pastor for many of those who are renowned, is well acquainted with the celebrity life style. What does he feel are some of their other problems?

> Another thing I think is a major problem of those in the entertainment community who are believers is

the death-dealing quest of the Christian community to exploit these people. They are often like vultures, preying on a "star" for entrepreneurial purposes. We *are* committed to seeing each of their ministries spread, so my feelings do not reflect some clutchy jealousy on my part as a pastor or on our part as a congregation to keep them "in house," so to speak. I am, instead, troubled by the motivation behind the inviting of these people into ministry situations. Much of it is unworthy, and I don't think the people recognize it. I don't think they are conscious of it. There is a slavering after fame that really belies an underlying carnality and violation of biblical principles and sensitivity.

For example, James says, "If you say to the rich man, 'Come and sit here,' " that preferred treatment by reason of position is wrong. And that is exactly what is often done, rather than simply loving the celebrity as a brother or sister. The spiritually newborn ones especially need a time to grow up. Otherwise, the person's spiritual life is virtually prostituted. When people ask me if a person is spiritually ready to appear somewhere, I appreciate it. That kind of sensitivity reflects spiritual maturity. It gives these people a chance to mature too.

Hayford explains how Christians can often stunt the spiritual growth of celebrities.

It is one thing to simply present a testimony of a person and another to talk about what the Lord is currently doing in his life. So many times when people want to platform a show personality as a Christian testimony, all they want to know is how the personality got saved. This ends up draining the celebrity of any opportunity for growth. Nobody expects him to grow. "Just tell us how you got

The Reverend Jack Hayford

saved. You are so neat." That is the kind of mentality I mean.

Besides dealing with outside problems, the Christian celebrity has to deal with inner problems such as pride, loneliness and ego.

> Those things at an internal, subjective level I'm sure would be a temptation to them. Human beings have trouble with pride. As a matter of fact, I don't find celebrities having as much trouble with pride as a lot of other people do. That wouldn't be true of all of them. They have been exposed to so much for so long that generally they know the shallowness of mere acclaim. They would have the same problems of pride in quest of status.

Hayford pinpoints the main problem that he sees.

> The thing that I find that is more of a concern is that the stars have terrible schedules. That's becoming increasingly common in our society too. So while it is not outstanding, it is usually a problem.
>
> There is one place where I think our church has helped many of these people who are sensitive to schedules. We happen to have resources in our congregation of media and ministries. We have a lot of people in the Christian—I don't like the word entertainment—in the traveling Christian ministries. What is true of one is generally true of the others in terms of travel and with our media resources; we keep in touch with them. We use the tape ministry. We go out of our way and we would do this for anyone else in the church even if he wasn't renowned, to service people who are itinerant in their lives. We strongly function in this respect and these people respond to this.
>
> All ministry must function out of relationship to

Celebrity Witness

the local assembly. We nourish that, believing God hasn't given them to us so we will be famous as the "church of the stars." God gave them to us for mutual exchange of ministry. We are heavy in our church on the emphasis of the ministry of every member of the body, so these folks have ministries. The schedules are bizarre for most of them.

There is another side to this issue, however.

There are some who are so used to special treatment as a star personality that to adjust to the discipline of plain, everyday spiritual growth is a very difficult thing for them.

How does Hayford recommend that Christians pray for their brothers and sisters who are celebrities?

I think the principal thing is to pray for them to have continued acceptance in their own community or enterprise. It is very easy for those around them to be either threatened or intimidated by word of their conversion, and if they do continue to accept them, they accept them on somewhat reserved terms. I think when these people have a chance to keep moving in the circles where they have been, there is the continued widespread witness of their lives where they are seen; but the really powerful thing is what happens that is never seen, with the people they deal with. They are not stories that are to be told. I know of a very long list of people of renown that have been touched by these celebrities, and the touch was not that those people came to the Lord right then, but that they were refreshed and renewed in attention to spiritual values. The difficult thing for them to get through at first was when it was heard that they were spiritually inclined, the people they work with did not know for sure how to relate to them.

The Reverend Jack Hayford

Hayford continues his advice.

> So, one point is to pray for acceptance and entrance for personal ministry. I think another thing is to pray for an anointing upon them to insulate them from the real attacks of the powers of darkness, because they are on the cutting edge of confrontation with the spirit of the world. The show community is as worldly as the world gets. It has its own kind of viciousness, and Satan will do anything that he can to discredit those people, though they be pure and faithful to Christ and His Word.
>
> Take Pat Boone, for example. He has been for so many years the picture of Mr. Clean. But the slightest thing he does will cause the news media to rise up to attack him. Suppose he makes a business misjudgment, which anyone could make. News reports will give it the sound of dishonesty. Pat's gone through quite a bit of flack like this. He has certainly kept his hands clean, but you certainly would have a hard time being sure of that to hear the press at times.
>
> We need to pray for insulation for these from the cruel works of darkness. Because of the schedules they carry, all of them need to be sensitive to their family life and their marriage, not because they are insensitive to family needs or that they are even tempted to unfaithfulness. It is neither of those things. It is just simply that the times they do have together would be quality and fruitful times.

Hayford makes some suggests for the Christian community.

> I would love to see Christian communities mature to the point that the use of celebrities in witness situations (television, rallies, etc.) really was motivated by a sense of Holy Spirit direction and not

Celebrity Witness

just by entrepreneurship. "Well, let's just get so-and-so." You don't really feel that people prayed over it. Just, "Who can we think of—some names who will draw a crowd?" It will take "this personality" to attract so many. It lacks a sense of Holy Spirit direction in it at all. It is just plain old showmanship. I wish that there were more spiritual sensitivity in that area. It would probably quit putting the kinds of pressure on the celebrities that they get.

19
Dorian Leigh

Dorian Leigh was cited as the top model of all time by Eileen Ford, head of the Ford Modeling Agency. Leigh was known as Revlon's "Fire and Ice" girl in the 1950s. The author of *The Girl Who Had Everything,* Leigh was known for her notorious life style. How does she describe her life style during that time?

> Well, it wasn't exactly jet-setting as most of my publicity has said, because I always had children. Wherever I settled, from Pennsylvania to Paris, I always took the children with me. That was the most important thing.

In spite of Dorian's financial status, she experienced some drawbacks with her kind of life style.

> I always had enough money. I worked hard, so I'd have enough money for a governess and people to take care of the house. I was really an absentee mother even though the children were in the same city with me. That was one of the biggest faults I had. I wanted to have them there, so I could love them, but they didn't have any mother to love.
>
> When I look at it now, I know that was wrong. I just wasn't there enough and no career woman is. It is a trade-off. Every man has to do it. Men are criticized

Celebrity Witness

because they give their lives to their careers and because of the competitive world; and they don't pay enough attention to their wives and their children, and the same thing happens to a woman. She has to choose and the children always suffer.

Dorian's life style has changed since she became a Christian a couple of years ago. Her first move was to turn over her modeling agency to someone else.

It really wasn't a question of selling it. I turned it over to someone else who could pay the debts that I owed to the models I had. She continued to give me 10 percent of the income of the models that I gave her and of the ones I discovered after that. She took the agency over, which was marvelous. As a matter of fact, the Germans and the Italians from time to time go through a wave of saying, "No more foreign models." They also try to charge for Social Security. Their advertising structures are different from what they were in France. They end up not paying it, but in France the government insists on your sending them every month 46 percent. They consider that the girls are salaried. They don't consider that they are paid a fee but that they are employees. On top of that, there is a service charge of 20 percent now. It was 22 percent in the beginning. This makes the fees of the models the highest. The girls get the lowest fee in Europe, but the state makes a great deal of money.

Civil Service makes more because the administration of all that money is enormous. Well, most of the agencies left, as well as the photographers and the top models. As it is now, the assemblage is a little longer than it was. The magazines don't cover the high fashion the way they used to. They go and photograph the clothes usually on the house models. Magazines just can't afford it.

Dorian Leigh

Dorian describes how the system in New York is different.

In New York, a model is an independent contractor. Actually, the government on foreign models insists that she pay her income tax before she leaves the country. The modeling agencies withhold for her; therefore, it makes it easier. They take out the 20 percent; the client pays 20 percent to the agency.

Has Dorian had any contact with the modeling industry since becoming a Christian?

I came back seven years ago to run Stewart, which is the second biggest agency in the U.S.A. I ran it for six months and then I stopped because of the competition which had become enormous. The man who ran Stewart was rather like me; he was an independent. He was not incorporated. He was using his own money to run his agency. And when Johnny Casablancas, Wilhelmina and Eileen all got into a big fight, he just couldn't keep up because they could afford to buy models away from him which they did. I said to him, "I don't see why you issue a head sheet (a head sheet is what the agencies issue showing what models they have) because most of the other agencies, as soon as a girl becomes famous, woo her away from Stewart." They were marvelous at discovering girls; but they all ended up at Eileen Ford, Casablancas or Wilhelmina because they wanted to be in a big name agency.

Has the modeling industry changed over the years?

It hasn't changed. Just as the model is under pressure—so are the agencies. Their methods have become rougher and rougher. It is no longer free-enterprise. It is free cut-throat. Of course, I'm still approached. When I go to speak about my books, people always come up and say, "I have a niece; I have a daughter; I have a sister and I'd like you to look at her pictures. Would you meet her and advise her about whether she should be a model?" And the main reason I can't have anything more to do with the modeling business is that I cannot say to the girl, "I think you should be a model." I think she'd love making all that money, but I do think it is dangerous. I really can't advise any young girl to be a model.

I still have the reflex when I see a beautiful girl to think, "Oh, she would be marvelous," or even a girl who isn't beautiful when I realize, from looking at her, that she would photograph very well. I still have to tell myself that she is better off as she is.

Does Dorian think that a Christian girl could be a top model and committed to the Lord in today's society?

It is very difficult because the pressures are so much stronger than they were when I was a model. The competition is so much keener. When I began modeling, it was so little known as a profession that my mother and father felt that I couldn't use the name Parker. That is why I used the name Dorian Leigh, which is my middle name. They felt it was a disgrace. Then Susie came along. She was fifteen years younger than I. My parents decided I hadn't really started walking the streets, so they let Susie use the name Parker.

Getting back to the issue on whether a girl can be a committed Christian and be a model—I would find it extremely difficult. There is an exception in this business and a great exception. A man named Paul Marionnet, who is the art director of *House and Garden* in Paris. He was art director of *House and Garden* here for many years before he went back to Paris. He is a Christian. He has a ministry. He

Dorian Leigh

preaches in what they call in France a temple, because the church, any church is automatically Catholic. So they label Protestant churches as temples. He does have an evangelistic meeting every Sunday. That is proof of the strong faith he has because he has worked in Condé Nast, which I would say is one of the greatest snakepits. The competition there among the editors, among the staff, is as bad as it is between the models and the modeling agencies.

What is the modeling industry like now?

The sums of money are so much greater because of television. Every job is negotiated. Before, you had a fee of sixty dollars per hour and it didn't matter what you were doing unless you were modeling underwear and then the fee was $120 per hour. But now, make-up publicity and advertising pays much, much more because you cannot pose freely. If you do a national ad, no other make-up company wants to use you because you'd be identified. Their advertising now is so incredibly widespread that you become known for that ad and it was only after Susie worked for Revlon, that Revlon decided to make girls exclusive like Lauren Hutton.

Lauren Hutton gets a lot of publicity because of the sums of money involved. Because of this amount of money, these girls are subjected to the attention of people who are unscrupulous, who float in that half world of money, of publicity, propaganda, etc.

It is very difficult for the girls to keep their heads. They are told so many times how beautiful they are. Then, of course, because every single day, no matter how beautiful you are, how high you are in the modeling world, you are rejected in one way or another. Every day you meet another beautiful girl

Celebrity Witness

and you think, "She is more beautiful than I am." Just the uncertainty of it, the insecurity of it drives these girls if they have no other security, in other words, the inner security which Christ should bring them. They give under the pressure and there are the drugs. Of course, thirty years ago, drugs weren't as accessible. No one would have dreamed of it. We were afraid even to have a cold because it made the client so upset. You are obliged to be in good health all the time. It was only after I had my agency in Europe that I found girls arriving late, badly dressed, badly made-up because they were on drugs. A great many of those girls vanished because of the drugs.

Part V

Analysis and Conclusions

20
An Analysis of the Findings

As we consider the many points of view that have been shared, there are certain underlying concepts that most of the celebrities seem to agree upon. There are five main areas that have been investigated:

1. The effects of fame on a celebrity's life;
2. Their greatest needs;
3. Their views on marriage and the family;
4. Prevailing attitudes and problems, and
5. How decisions are made.

Although not every celebrity addressed each area, the following comments express what many of the celebrities interviewed had to say.

A. Effects of Fame

Bob Turnbull:
"Because we were from Hollywood or something, people would get fired up. It's a temptation to strut around, be your own person, to begin to think more highly of yourself than you should."

Celebrity Witness

Lauren Chapin:
"I didn't expect Hollywood to turn its back on me. I had no idea how to adjust to society, to ordinary, everyday living."

Nick Benedict:
"I didn't handle the fame very well. Even though I was popular and all that, I still wasn't real happy."

Bob Munger:
"I've always been successful. I would say that my success has tended to hold me a bit in awe."

Susan Howard:
"It hasn't been easy. It has been very difficult because it is such a popular show and there are so many people involved in it, so many egos involved in it, so much pressure from everything. There is a tendency, at times, to get caught up in it."

Jeannie C. Riley:
"People expected me to be in my little miniskirts and boots with my cleavage showing all the time.... Even then, I didn't want that kind of image, but I was helpless to do anything about it."

Reba Rambo:
"The worst thing is that a lot of people tend to put you on a pedestal. It is difficult to establish any kind of long-term relationships."

Cheryl Blackwood:
"I don't feel any different now than I felt when I was teaching school. I have not changed any of the part of me that's really me. I've grown up and I'm older and I think maybe a little differently. But I feel the same way.

An Analysis of the Findings

I'm just dealing with a little more cash, but I do it the same way I did before."

Andrae Crouch:
"It is really rough on a person when they're popular because some people see you only as a song, not as a person."

Art Linkletter:
"For me, it has made me more aware of my responsibility as an example."

Graham and Treena Kerr:
1. They were worth millions of dollars.
2. Their program was seen around the world, and millions of people were watching them.
3. They had every materialistic need in the world except a good relationship with their children and with each other.
4. Treena was a drug addict and was able to support her habit.

Jack Hayford:
"We do not attract people who are looking for a show. A lot of entertainers just want the opportunity to be a human being."

Dorian Leigh:
"It is very difficult because the pressures are so much stronger than they were when I was a model. The competition is so much keener."

B. Greatest Needs

Bob Turnbull:
"The best area is to pray for God's perfect will in their life . . . that entertainers know how to wisely use their funds and that they be protective of their private time."

Celebrity Witness

Lauren Chapin:
"I'd pray for wisdom in all things! That when I go to minister, I would be wise in leading God's children into all truth, into salvation and beyond salvation into a daily commitment and walk with Christ."

Nick Benedict:
"I would ask God to give me another chance. Because I wouldn't make the mistakes that I made before. I've been praying for a second chance to break the bondage because Satan had a hold of me out in Los Angeles."

Johnny Zell:
"My greatest need is to be unselfish, more unselfish than I've ever been and to be very content with exactly what I am doing."

Danniebelle Hall:
"I'd like to be like a finely tuned instrument that the Lord can just choose to play at any time and that I'd be in tune whenever He decides to use me."

Reba Rambo:
"To have the wisdom of God from God."

Terry Blackwood:
"We would desire the mind of Christ, wisdom and understanding to know what the voice of God is. When He's speaking; when to move; to have the mind of Christ in every decision that we make."

Art Linkletter:
"The prayers to sustain me in my efforts is what I need."

Jack Hayford:
"I think the principal thing is for them [celebrities as individual human beings] to have continued acceptance in their own community or enterprise."

An Analysis of the Findings

C. Marriage and the Family

Lauren Chapin:
"If I ever get married, hopefully I'll have a home like Jim and Margaret. Because that is what I want. I want that white picket fence. I want the family working out problems together as a nucleus, not singly. I just want that love that flows back and forth."

Nick Benedict:
"I've been thinking a lot about fatherhood lately. To create a life, to carry on the family name. I'm ready for it."

Rita McLaughlin Walter:
"We're going to be celebrating our eighth year in December [1984], because God has told us to esteem each other greater than ourselves."

Johnny Zell:
"We've learned together that marriage is more important in life, above your work or anything. We'd get out of the music business in a minute if it was affecting our marriage."

Noel Paul Stookey:
Noel realized that his main ministry was to his family. Family became his top priority instead of making money.

Danniebelle Hall:
"Unless you are traveling together, husband and wife or kids, I think you are going to run into problems."

Cheryl Blackwood:
"I think that, first and foremost, the thing that should be said and done for every Christian marriage to stay

Celebrity Witness

together is for the husband and wife to put their marriage above everything else in their lives: Their ministries, their careers, even their families and friends. Nothing should go above their marriage."

Art Linkletter:
"She gives me the other side. After the shock of public adulation, she keeps me on a level keel."

Graham and Treena Kerr:
"The one thing that was specifically alive was the desire to remain together."

"Ephesians 5: Some of the most important words in that Bible verse are that man nourishes and cherishes his wife as he does his own body."

Dorian Leigh:
"I wasn't there and no career woman is. The children always suffer."

D. Attitudes and Problems

Efrem Zimbalist, Jr.:
"It is all right to enjoy an entertainer, but to worship him is really being misled."

Bob Turnbull:
"You prostitute yourself in interviews where you're selling yourself. You become aware of your own talents. You become your own god."

Lauren Chapin:
"I think struggling with breaking away from that identity of Kathy Anderson and having people see me as Lauren Chapin. Kathy can be a thorn in my side sometimes."

An Analysis of the Findings

Rita McLaughlin Walter:
"For some reason, people in churches think that somehow God doesn't care about people who work in television."

Bob Munger:
Bob has received criticism for his films dealing with the power of the antichrist. He says, "If you want to reach the unsaved people, you are going to be subject to criticism by the people who are really shortsighted."

Susan Howard:
"I've had it asked of me by Christians how I could do a show like *Dallas.* I don't worry about answering it anymore. I'm where I should be. I have peace within.

"The majority of actors and actresses are very insecure human beings. This is because your life style is based on what somebody else judges you to be. You are either too fat for this role or too thin—too tall, too old. You're white or black or green or yellow or whatever it happens to be. You are constantly up for grabs, as it were, to somebody else's opinion."

Joan Winmill Brown:
Joan feels that in Hollywood, Christian actors and actresses can easily be overwhelmed because of a Christian's sensitive and vulnerable nature.

Jeannie C. Riley:
"It was very hard becoming a Christian in show business, with an already established image which was derogatory to the things I now represent. There had to be a visible change. People are threatened by that kind of change. Christianity represents such a sacrifice to them. It's going to cost somebody something. That's all they seem to think about."

Celebrity Witness

Johnny Zell:
"Just trusting Him and knowing Him much better, the problems don't seem to stay around that long."

Noel Paul Stookey:
As far as Noel is concerned, other entertainers did not really accept his life style when he became a Christian. He says, "They didn't take me seriously. I think, conditionally, they kept waiting for me to come off of it."

Danniebelle Hall:
"When people put you up—emulate you—you realize what a tremendous responsibility you have. I felt very bound in this position."

Reba Rambo:
"So many people I've been around make it a point of keeping me humble."

Art Linkletter:
"I realized that there were so many good things to talk about and so much fun on a high level, why risk offending anybody?"

Jack Hayford:
"A thing I think is a major problem of believers in the entertainment community is the death-dealing quest of the Christian community to exploit these people."

Dorian Leigh:
"Because of the amount of money, these girls are subject to the attention of people who are unscrupulous."

An Analysis of the Findings

E. Decision Making

Efrem Zimbalist, Jr.:
"I don't have control over a movie. All I have is the ability to say I will accept this role or I won't accept this role. I would rather build than destroy."

Bob Turnbull:
Bob leaves himself open to God's direction in his career. His goal is to bring others to Christ. As he puts it, "The method of getting them there may vary, but the message is the same. We shouldn't be so critical of other people's methods, especially if the Lord's in charge."

Lauren Chapin:
Lauren talks about the kinds of films that she would consider doing: "Number one—it would not be a film that had a lot of sex or violence in it. It would not be a horror film. It would have to be family oriented, a 'G' rating."

Nick Benedict:
"I think the lessons I've learned will give me more guidelines for my life. I'm not necessarily concerned about the roles I play as long as I work as an actor. I would never go on something that was pornographic or anything like that."

Rita McLaughlin Walter:
"Now as long as they [that is, the movie's theme] say that sin is wrong, I can play a robber in a movie—as long as the cops win."

Bob Munger:
"The problem you get is the distortion of the biblical message. There are some gross distortions which I try to keep out of pictures that I'm involved with."

Celebrity Witness

Joan Winmill Brown:
"I feel that actors and actresses, and anyone that is in the media, have such a responsibility to portray the right kind of role."

Jeannie C. Riley:
"In entertainment, more than any other business, there's this thing [an expectation from people that leads to great pressure] that if you've become a Christian, why didn't you drop every single, solitary, secular song that you sing and sing only gospel? I won't sing something unscriptural, but that doesn't mean that I have to sing *all* Scripture."

Noel Paul Stookey:
"I retired from secular shows in 1970 and worked sporadically after that, and really work on a limited basis now. So when I *do* work, it's primarily to evangelize one way or the other."

Danniebelle Hall:
"I see that I'm going to be involved in the business part of the ministry a lot more than I am now."

Art Linkletter:
"I will not play any part or participate in any program which is demeaning, immoral or cheap or represents me as anything other than a reasonably nice, constructive person."

Reba Rambo:
"I do some secular concerts . . . . I just pick positive message tunes that aren't real preachy . . . . My main dream is to reach the world . . . I have to open my own mail from God for my own ministry."

21
Conclusions

There are many statements which can be made that reflect the true heartfelt desire and attitude of the Christian celebrity. In the previous interviews, it is obvious that there are many common denominators that provide a basis for comparison. The Christian celebrity life style is one that presents a unique set of opportunities as well as problems.

When a person receives the stature that fame brings, there is a tendency to become prideful. Ego is always a problem until the well-known person puts his fame into perspective. This status can be easily misused for selfish purposes. Fame can fade as quickly as it appears, and even though it does have its financial rewards, money soon ceases to satisfy inner needs.

Spiritually, the celebrity who is a Christian recognizes his responsibility to represent Christ in a worthy manner. This new responsibility often causes the celebrity to seek Christ in a greater way than before.

It is difficult for a Christian celebrity when he is not regarded as a human being by others. He is often put up and idolized, and this is very damaging. He often wonders if people like him for what he is or for who he is. Some of the Hollywood casting directors shy away from hiring those who have made an overt witness for Christ. The Christian celebrity who received fame from the secular world will often be welcomed with open arms from Christian circles.

Celebrity Witness

The celebrities interviewed realized that they had to live in the world, yet not become a part of it. Because of this, most of them do not reject secular jobs or appearances. They view this as an opportunity to share Christ with those who have not heard the gospel.

For the actors, they will take a role in secular productions as long as the role condemns evil and uplifts truth or Christian values. They will even portray an evil character as long as this condition is met. Overall, the actors will not play a part in anything that is demeaning or immoral. They consider a role as a job, not as a license to preach.

It is obvious that most actors consider the scripting and intent of a role before accepting or rejecting it. The ultimate effect that the role would have over the viewing audience is just as important as the morality of the role itself. In most cases, the actors realized the tremendous influence they exerted over admirers and knew that they had a tremendous responsibility to project the right image.

The musicians interviewed seek to project wholesome values through their lyrics. Most of them participate in secular productions. It is often said that music speaks in every language. This was proven true a few years ago with Debby Boone's hit song, "You Light Up My Life." This song reached virtually the entire world. Few films or television shows can boast comparable world-wide appeal. As film producer Bob Munger said, "Most people today don't realize that the record business is about a $20 billion business and the film business is about a $3 billion business." Obviously the general public is investing a lot of money in the music business, and Christians are provided with a tremendous opportunity to witness through this medium.

The talk show host is different from most television personalities because the star portrays himself. The host is not usually considered to be an actor. His actions are his own and not those of another character. The talk show host is usually seen as a credible figure. His position implies that he

Conclusions

is an authority on what he presents. With this in mind, it's important that the talk show host nurture his image.

All celebrities interviewed had definite convictions about their involvement in their profession. They don't make compromises commitment-wise, yet their values are their own and it is difficult when someone else tries to put convictions on them.

In most cases, the celebrities realized that their greatest opposition comes from other Christians. This often hurts the Christian celebrity a great deal when he realizes that his brothers and sisters in Christ do not support his efforts. The detrimental effect is magnified when it is known that both groups are working toward the same ultimate goal. Various methods influence the public and it appears that a lot of time and effort is wasted over differences of opinion. As Bob Turnbull commented, "The methods of bringing people to Christ may vary, but the message is the same."

Criticism is hard for the celebrity to accept, particularly if judgments are made with a lack of knowledge. Oftentimes the celebrities themselves are the only ones who will defend themselves. When they realize how the Lord is using them in their professions, they try to ignore others' opinions and hold to their convictions. Along with criticism comes unrealistic demands and expectations. Since the celebrities are highly visible, other Christians expect them to be perfect in every aspect, rather than accept them as human beings.

Most interviewed realized that they can use their secular platform to reach people who otherwise would not hear the gospel. Although they do not usually try to preach in secular situations, they realize that a secular following will eventually become aware of their religious convictions. It is often felt that Christians outside the profession do not value talent like the non-Christian does. This lack of appreciation is discouraging to the celebrity who wants to follow God and have fellowship with others in the faith. Onlookers usually see the glamour involved rather than the hard work.

Celebrity Witness

It is obvious that those with celebrity status are living in a "glass house." Every action they make is carefully scrutinized or criticized. Although fame denotes acceptance and approval, it appears that the Christian celebrity is criticized by outsiders. It is unlikely that this situation will ever change. No one can measure up to everyone's standards.

Although basic human nature may not change, the situation that the Christian celebrity has to deal with can be improved. When the Christian community becomes more open-minded to the Christian celebrity and his role in the body of Christ, their perspective may become healthier. As Christians iron out petty differences concerning methods of witnessing, they will come closer to the ultimate goal of all Christians—bringing others into the kingdom of God.

22
Final Comments

Everyone longs to be special, to know that he has a contribution that only he can offer to the world. Whether you're a celebrity or not, it's important to realize that every person is created by God with his own uniqueness and that alone makes him special. It's not what he's given by the world, it's what he is inside.

Fame is not what makes you important. It's your ability to understand and do what is right. Motives are all important, because God looks more at the heart than anything else. After all, where your heart is, there you will find your treasure. Make sure your heart is set on something worthwhile and of lasting and eternal value. Setting your desire on the Lord will make you more of a success than anything else this life has to offer.

Worldly fame is often fleeting and most often catches people by surprise. Those who seek after it are usually not the ones who receive it. In the final result, it is the inherent character traits of a person that will endure. The stuff real men and women are made of is the only thing that will maintain a person's strength and dignity during times of defeat and unpopularity.

When we consider those who are idolized and emulated by the world and bear the name of Christ, it is imperative that we uphold these representatives of the kingdom of God in prayer. Those Christians who are in strong positions of influence

Celebrity Witness

have been given an enormous responsibility to live their lives in an unreproachable manner. Every word or action is usually scrutinized and most probably criticized. Would the rest of us be able to measure up under the watchful eyes of the world?

Intercessors carry the lifebeat of the work of God around the world. True, it's not a very glamorous position, but it's one of the most crucial in the kingdom of God. Those who would be great in the kingdom of God are the servants of all. Is there any more appropriate example of servanthood than that of those who spend their time before the throne of God in intercession for us all?

So, whatever your calling, it's important to be the best you can be for our Lord Jesus Christ so that we might glorify Him with our entire being. And, if God places you in a prominent position of influence, rejoice and know that He will be there to guide you in all wisdom and truth. Our only requirement is obedience as we listen to that still, small voice of God.